Bead & Wire Jewelry for Special Occasions

Bead & Wire Jewelry for Special Occasions

Linda Jones

35 STEP–BY–STEP PROJECTS FOR BIRTHDAYS, WEDDINGS, VALENTINE'S DAY, MOTHER'S DAY, AND MORE

CICO BOOKS

LONDON NEW YORK

Dedication

I would like to dedicate this book with love to my special partner, Chris, who continues to pour countless riches into my life and provides me with the space to evolve with my passion for jewelry design.

Published in 2007 by CICO Books
an imprint of Ryland Peters & Small
519 Broadway, 5th Floor, New York NY 10012

10 9 8 7 6 5 4 3 2 1

Text and project designs copyright © Linda Jones 2007
Design and photography copyright © CICO Books 2007

A CIP catalog record for this book is available from the Library of Congress

ISBN-13: 978 1 906094 01 0
ISBN-10: 1 906094 01 2

Printed in China

Editor: Sarah Hoggett
Designer: David Fordham
Photographer: Geoff Dann
Stylist: Sammie Bell

Contents

Introduction 6

Tools & Techniques 9
  Tools 10
  Materials 11
  Basic techniques 14

Valentine's Day 25
  Cupid's love chain 27
  Sweetheart necklace 30
  Lover's knot bracelet 35
  Lover's ring 38
  Love eternal necklace 43

Mother's Day 47
  Beaded scarf slide 48
  Flower cuff 53
  Wiggly chain 56
  Bow pin 61

Birthdays 65
  Birthstone bracelet 66
  Birthstone necklace 71
  Tassel clip 74
  Flower pin 79

Weddings 83
  Bride's tiara 84
  Pearly necklace 89
  Bridal hair grip 92
  Bridesmaid's necklace 97
  Bridesmaid's wand 100

Christmas 105
  Christmas star pendant 107
  Holly-leaf necklace 110
  Beaded bauble pendant 115
  Christmas wreath necklace 118
  Christmas tree earrings 123

Suppliers 126
Index 127
Acknowledgments 128

Introduction

There are special occasions in all our lives that we want to mark with something unique and symbolic—and what better way than to create a stunning gift, or make your own jewelry especially for that day?

This book contains a range of jewelry designs for some of the most memorable celebrations throughout the year—Valentine's Day, Mother's Day, birthdays, weddings, and Christmas. All the designs can be made without any prior jewelry-making experience, although I recommend that you read and practice all the basic techniques in the first section to gain knowledge of your tools, materials, and essential wire-working techniques.

I've tried to keep to the spirit of each occasion by using, for example, romantic heart-shaped motifs for several of the Valentine's Day projects, semi-precious birthstones for the birthday pieces, and traditional decorative motifs such as Christmas trees and holly leaves for Christmas—

but of course, many of the designs would suit more than one celebration. The Mother's Day Beaded Scarf Slide on page 48, for example, would also make a wonderful birthday or Christmas gift, and the Sweetheart Necklace on page 30 would be fabulous as a wedding choker.

ABOVE
This matching necklace and earring set was made using chip stones of semi-precious amethyst, the birthstone for the month of February.

In this age of mass production, it can be difficult to find something original to purchase, especially in costume jewelry. I hope that my designs will inspire you to create your own unique jewelry pieces. Use them as a starting point: change the bead colors and wire gauges, mix and match elements of the projects together, or adapt the designs to suit your unique personality and style. Above all, use them as a way of celebrating memorable events by creating timeless jewelry with much thought and love!

LINDA JONES

ABOVE
A sparkling tiara, guaranteed to make every bride feel like a princess—and surely the ultimate piece of special-occasion jewelry!

Tools & Techniques

The next few pages provide a brief overview of the main tools and materials needed for making wire and beaded jewelry, along with the basic techniques you will need. You may well be surprised to discover just how little you need in the way of specialist skills and equipment. The thrill of jewelry making, for most people, lies in selecting from the vast array of beads and wires on offer: from semi-precious stones and hand-made glass beads to mass-produced beads, there really is something to suit every occasion.

LEFT
Just a few of the many kinds of beads on offer. When you're buying
materials, make sure they suit the recipient's personality and style,
so that they cherish the piece of jewelry and wear it often!

ools

One of the joys of making wire and beaded jewelry is that you require very little in the way of specialist tools and equipment. The items shown on these two pages are virtually all you need and all are readily available from craft suppliers, mail-order catalogs, and, of course, the Internet.

Pliers and cutters

The only really essential pieces of equipment are a good pair of wire cutters and two or three kinds of pliers with which to shape the wire. There are three types of pliers used in making wire jewelry—round-nose, flat-nose, and chain-nose. As pliers and cutters are tools that you will use all the time, it is well worth investing in good-quality products.

ROUND-NOSE PLIERS have round, tapered shafts, around which you bend the wire–so they are ideal for coiling and bending wire into small loops and curves, as well as for making jump rings to link units together.

FLAT-NOSE PLIERS have flat, parallel jaws. They are used to grip the wire firmly as you work with it, and to bend it at right angles. They are also essential for neatening and flattening ends so that no sharp wires stick out. Unlike household electrical pliers, they are smooth-jawed, with no serrations or grips that might mark the wire. This is particularly important for enamel-coated, colored wires, because if the coating is damaged you will be able to see the copper wire core underneath, which would spoil the look of the piece.

CHAIN-NOSE PLIERS are similar to flat-nose pliers, but they have tapered ends. They are useful for holding very small pieces of wire and for fabricating more intricate and delicate pieces, as well as for bending angular shapes in wire.

WIRE CUTTERS are available in several forms, but I find that "side cutters" are the most useful as they have small, tapered blades that can cut into small spaces. Always hold the cutters perpendicular to the wire when cutting to achieve a clean cut.

From left to right: round-nose pliers, flat-nose pliers, chain-nose pliers, wire cutters.

Hammer and flat steel stake

These tools are used to flatten and toughen wire motifs (see page 21). You can use almost any HAMMER, provided it has a smooth, flat steel end, although specialist jewelry hammers are generally small and lighter than general-purpose household hammers, so you may find them easier to use.

A jewelry hammer and steel stake, used to flatten and work harden wire motifs (also see page 19).

STEEL STAKES can be bought from specialist jewelry stores. The surface must be polished smooth, otherwise the wire will pick up any irregularities that are present. Always keep the hammer head at right angles to the wire being hit, otherwise you will obtain a textured surface.

Mandrel

To form circular shapes such as rings and bangles, you will need a MANDREL. You can buy purpose-made mandrels in varying sizes; alternatively, shape your wire around any cylindrical object of the appropriate size. Wooden dowels from your local home-improvements store are an inexpensive option. Depending on the size you need, you could also improvize by wrapping wire around a round-barrelled pen, a glass jar or bottle, a rolling pin, or a curtain pole.

Top: A specialist ring mandrel, marked with gradations showing standard ring sizes. Bottom: an improvized mandrel—a short length of wooden dowel.

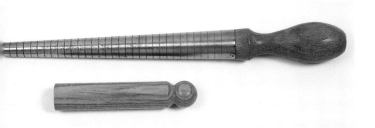

Materials

There is such a wonderful array of beautiful beads, colorful wires, and findings that you will be spoilt for choice! When you're making a piece of jewelry to celebrate a special occasion, however, some materials spring to mind immediately. Gold and silver wires—either plated or made entirely from the precious metal—always look luxurious, particularly for a once-in-a-lifetime occasion such as a wedding. Similarly, pearls (for weddings) and semi-precious chip stones (for birthdays or anniversaries) are obvious choices. But of course, it all depends on the occasion—and, just as importantly, on the age and personality of the person for whom you're making the piece.

Wire

WIRE is available in many thicknesses, types, and colors. Colored, copper, and plated wires can be bought from most craft and hobby stores, as well as from bead suppliers. Colored wires are usually copper based with enamel coatings, which means that they must not be hammered or over-manipulated as this might remove the surface color.

With the exception of precious metal, wire is generally sold in spools of a pre-measured length. Precious-metal wire is bought by length, the price being calculated by weight. Always store precious-metal wire in self-seal bags, away from

Colored wires are available in every color of the rainbow!

All these kinds of wire come in different thicknesses. Depending on where you buy your wire, different measurements are used to denote the thickness of the wire. The chart below will enable you to convert quickly from one system to another. The most commonly used general-purpose wire is 20-gauge (0.8 mm).

28-gauge	0.4 mm	Binding, knitting, and weaving
24-gauge	0.6 mm	Threading small delicate beads; binding and twisting
20-gauge	0.8 mm	General-purpose jewelry work
18-gauge	1.0 mm	Chunkier pieces and ring shanks
16-gauge	1.2 mm	Bolder, chunkier jewelry
14-gauge	1.5 mm	Very chunky, metallic wire jewelry

oxygen, to prevent it from tarnishing. If it does look dull, rub it with a soft polishing cloth.

Instead of precious-metal wires, I almost always use gold- or silver-plated wires, which are far less expensive and, in the case of silver-plated, will not tarnish so quickly. The only exception to this is if you need to file the wire (as in the Bow Pin on page 61), as filing will expose the copper core underneath the coating. Therefore, sterling-silver wire is essential for this particular design.

Beads

BEADS are made from all kinds of materials including glass, porcelain, plastic, metal, wood, and bone. Specialist bead stores contain literally thousands of different sizes and types, arranged by both color and size, and I defy

Glass beads range from completely transparent to almost opaque. They can be expensive, particularly if they are made from hand-blown glass, so they are perhaps best used as "focal" beads for maximum impact.

Copper-, gold-, and silver-plated wires are less expensive than the precious-metal versions but look just as convincing.

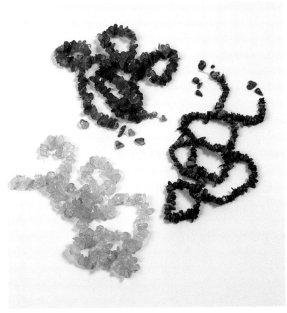

Seed beads are usually sold in small tubes. They are useful as "stopper" beads but, because they are so tiny, if you want them to have any impact in a design you generally need to string several together. The size of a seed bead refers to the number that will fit into 1 in. (2.5 cm) when laid end to end—so the higher the number, the smaller the bead.

Semi-precious chip stones are sold in 16- or 18-in. (40- or 45-cm) lengths. When you are ready to use them, snip the thread that holds them together and store the beads in small containers. Again, these are lovely beads to use for jewelry for special occasions such as birthdays and anniversaries, as you can match the bead to the recipient's birthstone and create a piece that is not only aesthetic, but also symbolic.

anyone to visit such a store without buying a selection!

Always check that the wire you are using fits through the bead hole, as there is no correlation between the size of a bead and the diameter of its hole. If you can't find beads that match those used in the projects in this book, buy something of a similar size. You will also find that many bead suppliers sell mixed colored bead bags at wholesale prices. These are often great value!

embellishments. Ready-made jump rings, fasteners, and head pins can bought from suppliers, but you can create your own by following the step-by-step instructions in the basic techniques section, using wire that matches the rest of your project.

Findings

FINDINGS is the jewelry term used to describe ready-made components such as chains, ear wires, fasteners, and so on. They can be bought from craft and hobby stores. If you are using a ready-made chain in a design, check that the links are large enough to take whatever thickness of wire you use to thread or suspend the

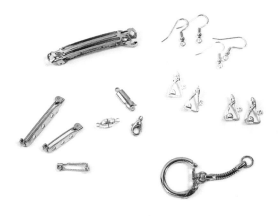

Ready-made findings come in a wide variety of colors and finishes.

Basic techniques

If this is your first attempt at wire jewelry, practice all the basic techniques to become familiar with the fundamentals of wire working and get a "feel" for your main ingredient—wire.

Threading beads with wire

The basic principle is to construct a neat loop of wire (known as a "link") at each end of the bead, which is then used to suspend the bead from a chain or to connect one bead to another.

1 Working from the spool, thread your chosen bead onto the wire, leaving about ½ in. (1 cm) of wire extending on each side of the bead with which to form the link.

2 Remove the bead and cut the wire with your wire cutters.

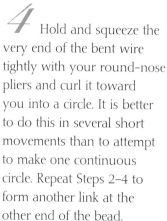

4 Hold and squeeze the very end of the bent wire tightly with your round-nose pliers and curl it toward you into a circle. It is better to do this in several short movements than to attempt to make one continuous circle. Repeat Steps 2–4 to form another link at the other end of the bead.

3 Thread the bead back onto the cut wire. Holding the wire vertically, with the bead in the center, use the tips of your round-nose pliers to bend the wire at a right angle, at the point where it touches the bead.

At the end, hold each link firmly in the jaws of your pliers and twist until both links face the same way.

Making a head pin

If you want to suspend a bead from a chain, you only need a suspension link at one end of the bead. At the other end, you need to make what is known as a "head pin," which is virtually invisible but prevents the bead from slipping off the wire.

The head pin is unobtrusive but prevents the bead from slipping off the wire.

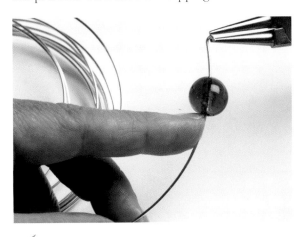

1 Working from the spool, thread your chosen bead onto the wire and let it slip down, leaving the end exposed.

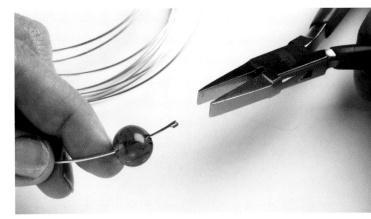

2 Using the tips of your round-nose pliers, make a tiny curl at one end of the wire. Squeeze this curl flat with your flat-nose pliers to create a knob of wire.

3 Push your bead right up to the "head pin" and snip the wire leaving a stem of about ½ in. (1 cm) and form a link at the other end using your round-nose pliers. If the hole in the bead is large and it slips over the head pin, bend the head pin at a right angle, so that the bead sits on top of it like a tiny shelf. (Alternatively, slide on a small seed bead to act as a stopper.)

You can also make a decorative feature of the head pin. To do this, you need to leave a longer length of wire below the bead. From left to right: wire curled into a closed spiral; wire hammered into a "feather" shape; seed bead threaded onto the wire above the head pin.

Making spirals

There are two kinds of spiral—open and closed. Each is formed in the same way, the only difference being whether or not any space is left between the coils. Both types of spiral begin by curling a circle at the end of the wire.

In an open spiral, evenly spaced gaps are left between the coils.

A closed spiral is made in the same way, but has no gaps between the coils.

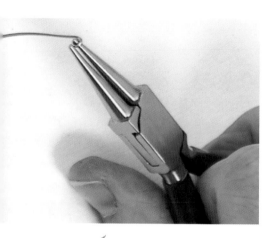

1 Begin by curling a small circle at the end of the wire, using the tips of your round-nose pliers. Make this circle as round as possible, as the rest of the spiral will be shaped around it.

2 Grip the circle tightly in the jaws of your flat-nose pliers and begin curling the wire around it. For a closed spiral, shown here, butt each coil up tightly against the previous one. For an open spiral, leave space between one coil and the next, making sure that the spaces are even.

3 When the spiral is the size you want, leave about ½ in. (1 cm) of wire to form a suspension link, curling the projecting end of wire into a small loop in the opposite direction to the spiral.

Making jump rings

Jump rings are used to connect units together. You can buy them ready made, but it is well worth learning how to make them yourself as you can then match the jump ring to the color and size of wire that you are using. It is also much less expensive to make them yourself!

Jump rings are made by forming a wire coil around the shaft of your round-nose pliers, out of which you snip individual rings as required. When you bring the wire around the pliers to

begin forming the second ring of the coil, it needs to go below the first coil, nearer your hand. This keeps the wire on the same part of the pliers every time. If you bring the wire round above the first ring of the coil, the jump rings will taper, following the shape of the pliers' shaft. You can also make jump rings by wrapping wire around a cylindrical object such as a knitting needle, a large nail or the barrel of a pen, depending on the diameter of jump ring that you require.

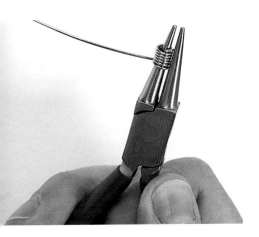
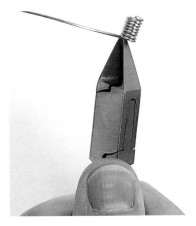

1 Working from the spool, wrap wire five or six times around one shaft of your round-nose pliers, curling it around the same part of the pliers every time to create an even coil.

2 Remove the coil from the pliers and cut it off the spool of wire using your wire cutters.

3 Find the cut end and, using your wire cutters, snip upward into the next ring of the coil, thereby cutting off a full circle. Continue cutting each ring off the coil in turn to obtain more jump rings.

Using jump rings to connect units

Using your flat-nose pliers, open one of the jump rings sidewise (like a door), so that you do not distort the shape. Loop the open jump ring through the links of the beads and close it with flat-nose pliers. To toughen (or work harden) the jump rings, carefully move the two ends of the ring just past one another (holding one side with your flat-nose and the other side with your chain-nose pliers); this will provide tension, enabling the cut ends to sit more securely together. Spend a little extra time checking that there are no gaps between your links, so that when you come to wear the piece you will know it won't all fall apart as the beads work themselves loose. (I speak from bitter experience!)

Jump rings can also be linked together to create a chain. From top to bottom: silver jump rings linked together; copper jump rings interspersed with pairs of smaller silver jump rings; copper jump rings.

Fish-hook clasp

The most commonly used clasp is the fish-hook, which is also one of the simplest to create.

This hook-shaped clasp is both decorative and functional.

1 Working from the spool, curl the end of the wire into a loop using your round-nose pliers. Reposition your pliers on the other side of the wire and curl the wire in the opposite direction to form the fish-hook clasp. Cut the wire off the spool, leaving about ½ in. (1 cm) extending, and form a link (see page 14).

2 If you wish, you can gently hammer the hook on a steel stake to work harden (see right) and flatten it slightly, thereby making it stronger and more durable.

Doubled fish-hook clasp

As a double thickness of wire is used, this fastener is much sturdier than a basic fish-hook clasp. You will need to cut at least 3 in. (7.5 cm) of wire.

1 Find the center of the wire and bend the wire around the tips of your round-nose pliers.

2 Using your round-nose pliers, squeeze the folded end of the wires together and straighten them out with your fingers, so that they run parallel to one another.

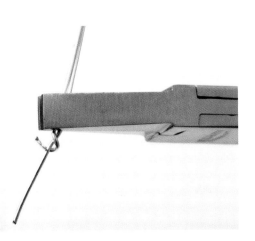

3 Leaving about 1 in. (2.5 cm) of doubled wire, wrap one wire two or three times around the other. Snip off any excess wrapped wire, leaving the other stem extending.

4 Curl the doubled wire around the shaft of your round-nose pliers into a hook shape. Again using your round-nose pliers, curl the tip of the hook up into a small "lip."

5 Complete the clasp by forming a link at the end of the single protruding wire. (For extra color and decoration, you can add a bead before forming your link.)

6 The double thickness of wire makes this a much sturdier clasp for necklaces and bracelets–particularly if they contain relatively heavy beads that might put a strain on an ordinary clasp.

Work hardening

To create wire jewelry without the aid of solder, you must know how to work harden, or toughen, your material so that it can take the strain of being worn without distorting or falling apart. One method is to hammer the piece on a steel stake. The stake must be clean, smooth and dent-free, or the wire will pick up irregularities.

Place your piece on the stake and "stroke" hammer it, ensuring that the flat part of the hammer comes down at 90° to the piece. It is easiest to hammer your piece standing up, as this ensures that the hammer head hits the wire squarely, rather than at an angle, which could creating texturing and "dimples" in the metal. After hammering the piece several times, you should notice the wire flattening and spreading.

Be careful when work hardening colored wire as the colored coating can rub off, exposing the copper core. Use a nylon hammer or place a cloth over the piece before hammering.

This technique is not suitable for small jump rings and links, as it will distort their shape. To strengthen jump rings, take one end in one pair of pliers and one end in another and gently push them just past the point at which they should join. Do this two or three times; the piece will be work-hardened just enough to hold the join without the aid of solder.

S-shaped clasp

If you'd like a clasp to look rather more decorative, an S-shaped clasp is a good option.

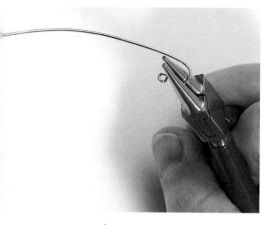

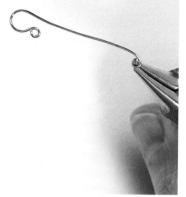

3 Place the widest part of your pliers just under the loop and mold the wire around the shaft in the opposite direction, to create a mirror image to the first curve and complete the "S" shape.

1 Working from the spool, curl a tiny loop at the end of the wire, using the tips of your round-nose pliers. Place the widest part of your pliers just under the loop and curve the wire in the opposite direction.

2 Cut the wire off the spool leaving a 1-in. (2.5-cm) stem. Make a small loop at the other end of the wire, curling toward the "hook" that you have just created at the other end.

A basic S-shaped clasp, which has been gently hammered to flatten and toughen it.

Adding a bead before you form the second curve of the S-shape makes an attractive variation. Wire it on each side with 28-gauge (0.4 mm) wire to prevent it from slipping.

The "eye" of the fastener

This "eye" can be used to complete all the clasps shown above.

1 Working from the spool, curl a piece of wire around the widest part of your round-nose pliers about 1 in. (2.5 cm) from the end of the wire to form a loop, crossing the end of the wire over itself.

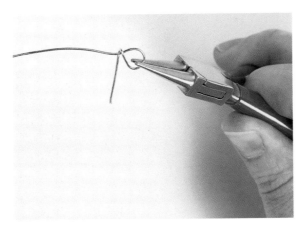

2 Wrap the extending wire around the stem, just under the loop, to secure. Squeeze the cut end flat against the stem with the tips of your chain-nose pliers, to ensure there are no spiky, protruding ends.

3 Cut the wire off the spool, leaving about ½ in. (1 cm) extending. Using the tips of your round-nose pliers, form the extending wire into a link (see page 14).

4 Gently hammer the rounded end of the "eye" on a steel stake to flatten and toughen it. Do not hammer the wires that have been wrapped over the stem or you will weaken them.

The completed "eye" of the fastener can be linked to the ends of a necklace or bracelet, either directly or via jump rings.

Neatening ends

When you've wrapped one piece of wire around another—as when making a clasp, for example—it's important to neaten the ends to prevent any sharp pieces from sticking out and snagging on clothing or scratching the wearer.

Simply snip the wire as close as possible to the stem, and then press it firmly with your flat- or chain-nose pliers to flatten it against the piece of jewelry.

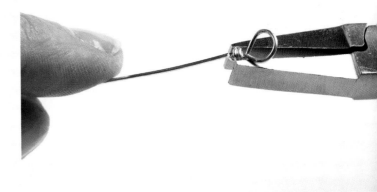

Beaded eye clasp

For a more decorative fastener, incorporate a bead in the "eye." You can use the same technique of wrapped loops when threading large beads to make the links more secure.

1 Working from the spool, thread your chosen bead onto the wire. About 1 in. (2.5 cm) from the end of the wire, bend the wire at right angles around the shaft of your round-nose pliers, so that it crosses over and forms a little loop.

2 Wrap the short end of the wire two or three times around the stem. Neaten the ends (see page 21).

3 Bend the wire at the other end of the bead at right angles, as in Step 1.

4 Wrap the wire around the shaft of the pliers to form another loop.

5 Holding the loop firmly in your flat-nose pliers, wrap the wire two or three times around the stem. Cut the wire off the spool and neaten the ends.

As a finishing touch, work harden the links (see page 19), taking great care not to hammer the bead.

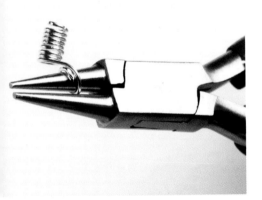

Coiled fish-hook clasp and fastener

This is a variation on the basic fish-hook clasp. It is used on cord, rope, or ribbon—in fact, on anything to which a jump ring or hook cannot be attached.

1 Working from the spool, make two coils of wire about ¼ in. (5 mm) long, in the same way as when making jump rings (see page 16). Remember to check that the cord or rope you are using can fit snugly into the center of the coil.

2 Cut the wire off the spool, leaving a 1-in. (2.5-cm) tail of wire on one coil and a 1½-in. (4-cm) tail on the other.

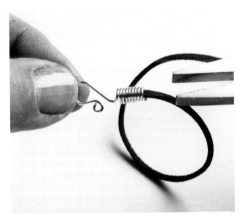

5 Insert the cord or ribbon into the coil. Press the last ring of the coil tightly against the cord with the tips of your flat-nose pliers, so that the fastener is held securely in place.

4 At the end of the shorter wire, curl your wire around the widest part of your round-nose pliers so that it sits perpendicular to the coil, thus forming the eye of the fastener.

3 At the end of the longer wire, form a fish-hook clasp (see page 18) without a suspension link. Using your flat-nose pliers, turn the hook at 90° to the coil.

The completed coiled fish-hook clasp and fastener. For added security, I recommend dabbing some Superglue just inside the end of the wire coil.

Chapter 1
Valentine's
Day

St Valentine's Day, 14 February, is a time for people to declare
their love. Whether you make the jewelry projects in this
chapter to give as a gift or to wear yourself for a
romantic night out, you'll find a range of timeless designs
to suit all ages, from the Cupid's Love Chain of interlocking hearts
on page 26 to the Love Eternal Necklace on page 42.

LEFT
These simple rings fit any finger size, as they are front opening.
Make them from just wire or choose a red bead (the color of love)
to add interest to the center.

Treat me to their heart's desire.
But by God's dear majesty
Such a death, I will not die,
Since I die, ah, better than to
Trust the boar than to
Choose all's evil, men trust then
Since all's evil, I the least."
Now they say and tell and
Nicolette made great sorrow.

...keeping, and fared on un...
...herself upon the fri...
...and she... little bear...
shepherds... lead their flocks...
spring, which... the river. The...
...the Greenwood... Nicolette,
laughing...

18

Cupid's love chain

You will need

20-gauge (0.8 mm) copper wire
Round- and flat-nose pliers
Wire cutters
Hammer and steel stake

The pinkish tone of the copper is intended to evoke Cupid, the chubby, pink cherub of love who strikes us with his loaded arrows just when we're least expecting it! This continuous chain-link design would work equally well as a bracelet. Alternatively, to make matching earrings, simply add delicate little beads to the heart-shaped units and suspend them from ready-made ear wires.

1 For a 16-in. (40-cm) chain, cut 18–20 pieces of 20-gauge (0.8 mm) copper wire 4–4½ in. (10–12 cm) long. Fold each wire in half. Squeeze the end of the doubled wires together with your flat-nose pliers and straighten out the wires with your fingers so that they run parallel to one another.

2 Using the tips of your round-nose pliers, curl a small loop at the doubled-over end of the wire, curling the wire toward you so that the loop is at right angles to the straight wires.

3 Holding the doubled loop firmly in your flat-nose pliers, gently pull the two wires apart.

LEFT
This delicate-looking chain looks great with all kinds of outfits, from a simple shirt to a dress for a more formal occasion.

Cupid's love chain

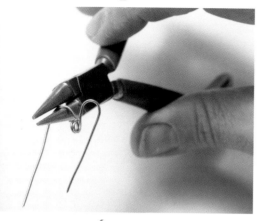

4 Place the widest part of your round-nose pliers on each side of the doubled loop and bring the wires back down until they meet and cross over, forming a heart-shaped frame.

5 Gently stroke hammer the round shoulders of the frame, taking care not to hammer and squash the doubled loop (see page 19).

6 Wrap one of the extending wires at the base of the heart two or three times around the other. Snip off any excess wrapped wire and squeeze the end flat against the stem with your flat-nose pliers to neaten, leaving the other wire extending.

7 Using your round-nose pliers, form a link (see page 14) at the end of the extending wire. Repeat Steps 1–7 to make 18–20 heart-shaped units.

8 Open the link at the base of one heart and loop it through the doubled-over loop of wire at the top of the next heart. Close the link again, using your flat-nose pliers.

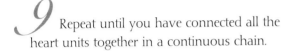

9 Repeat until you have connected all the heart units together in a continuous chain.

10 To complete the necklace, make a fish-hook clasp and a wrapped eye (see pages 18 and 20) from 20-gauge (0.8 mm) copper wire and attach to the ends of the necklace.

Variation

To make matching earrings, follow Steps 1–6 of the chain. Then, instead of forming a link at the base of the heart, thread one 3–4 mm bead onto the extending wire and form a spiral head pin (see page 15) at the end of the wire.

Thread another bead onto a 1-in. (2.5-cm) length 20-gauge (0.8 mm) copper wire, and form a link and one end and a head pin at the other (see page 15). Connect three jump rings together to form a small chain (see page 17), loop the top jump ring through the doubled loop at the top of the heart-shaped unit, and suspend the threaded bead from the bottom jump ring.

Sweetheart necklace

You will need

20-gauge (0.8 mm) silver wire

Approx. 60 x size 9/0 pink seed beads

1 x 7 mm pink bead

1 x 4 mm pink bead

2 x 16-in. (40-cm) lengths of ¼-in. (5 mm) pink ribbon

2 x 16-in. (40-cm) lengths of ¼-in. (5 mm) white ribbon

Wire cutters

Round- and flat-nose pliers

Mandrel or cylindrical dowel approx. ½ in. (1 cm) in diameter

Masking tape

Superglue

February is the time when sweethearts celebrate St Valentine's Day, so why not create a heart-shaped necklace and earring set to wear? This design can be made without beads, using a thicker gauge or colored wire, and suspended from a cord or chain for a more casual look. The heart motif would also look great on the front of a card or gift tag or attached to a key ring.

1 Cut a 6-in. (15-cm) length of 20-gauge (0.8 mm) silver wire. Holding the center with the ends of your round-nose pliers, curl the two ends of the wire around the shaft to form a loop.

RIGHT
Make matching earrings for a stylish jewelry set.

2 Place a mandrel or cylindrical dowel approximately ½ in. (1 cm) in diameter just by the central loop and bring the extending wires down on each side to form a heart shape.

3 Thread each side of the heart-shaped frame with size 9/0 pink seed beads, using approximately 30 beads on each side. Using your fingers, wrap one wire two or three times around the other at the base of the heart.

4 Snip off any excess wrapped wire and squeeze the end flat against the stem with your flat-nose pliers to neaten, leaving the other wire extending.

5 Thread a 7 mm pink bead onto the extending stem at the base of the heart-shaped frame and form a head pin (see page 15) to prevent it slipping off.

6 Cut a 6-in. (15-cm) length of 20-gauge (0.8 mm) silver wire. Place the tips of your round-nose pliers in the center and fold the wire in half.

7 Squeeze the end of the doubled wires together with your flat-nose pliers and straighten out the wires with your fingers so that they run parallel to one another.

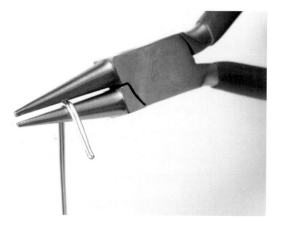

8 Place the shaft of your round-nose pliers about ½ in. (1 cm) from the end of the doubled-over wire and bend the wire around the pliers to form a hook.

Sweetheart necklace

9 Thread the doubled wire hook through the center loop of the heart frame and swivel the wires around the top of the heart, curling them around your round-nose pliers so that the wires are facing down.

10 Hold the hook firmly in the jaws of your flat-nose pliers and bend it upward, until it sits against the central loop.

11 Bend the extending wires down over the heart. Holding the hook firmly in your flat-nose pliers, form a tight spiral on one extending wire (see page 16), until you have only ½ in. (1 cm) of wire remaining. Make a second spiral on the other wire to mirror the first.

12 Thread a 4 mm pink bead onto 20-gauge (0.8 mm) silver wire, and form a head pin at one end and a link at the other (see page 15). Connect this bead to the central loop of the heart, so that it is suspended within the frame between the spirals.

13 Using a pink seed bead, make a beaded S-link and attach it to the doubled wire loop at the top of the heart frame.

14 Tape the four ends of the colored ribbons together and feed them through the top link of the S-link. Push the taped ends of the ribbons into coiled end clasps (see page 23) and secure with a tiny dab of Superglue.

Lover's knot bracelet

You will need

20-gauge (0.8 mm) silver wire

Heart-shaped, faceted beads about ½ in. (1 cm) long

Round- and flat-nose pliers

Wire cutters

Legend has it that Dutch sailors tied a knot to remind them of their loved ones during their long ocean voyages in the 16th century. The intertwining wire coils of this chain link symbolize two people intertwined in love. For a chunkier effect, use a thicker gauge of wire (18-gauge/1 mm) and link a chain of "knots" into a wrist band. You can adjust the length of this bracelet so that it sits tightly around the wrist, as you simply loop the hook into any link in the chain to close it.

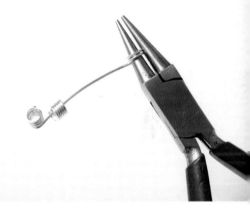

1 Working from a spool of 20-gauge (0.8 mm) silver wire, wrap the wire four or five times around one shaft of your round-nose pliers, curling it around the same part of the pliers every time to create an even coil about ½ in. (1 cm) long. Remove the coil from the pliers and cut it off the spool.

2 Pull more wire from the spool, thread the end through the coil, and create another coil in the same way as before, butting it right up against the first coil.

3 Cut the wire from the spool leaving approximately 2 in. (5 cm) projecting. Place your round-nose pliers at the end of the projecting wire and begin forming another coil.

LEFT
This bracelet is made using exactly the same technique as for making jump rings (see page 16).

Lover's knot bracelet

4 The third coil should sit tightly against the first coil, sandwiching it in the center. Neaten any spiky ends (see page 21).

5 For a bracelet approximately 7 in. (17 cm) long, make 11 or 12 coiled units. Make the required number of large jump rings (see page 16). Connect the coiled units together in a chain (see page 17) by looping jump rings through the end coils.

6 Make more jump rings and attach the heart-shaped beads to the bracelet, suspending them from alternate jump rings in the chain.

RIGHT
The coils of silver wire give this bracelet a very contemporary feel, and the colored crystal hearts really bring the bracelet to life. They are connected to alternate jump ring links between the "knot" units, each heart being suspended from a single link.

7 To complete the bracelet, make a doubled fish-hook clasp (see page 18) and attach it to one end of the bracelet. To close the bracelet, loop the clasp through any jump ring in the chain.

Variations

The gold-and-silver bracelet (left) has a timeless feel. For the earrings (above), bend the top and bottom rings of a coil at 90° and attach a bead and an ear wire.

Lover's ring

You will need

20-gauge (0.8 mm) and
  24-gauge (0.6 mm) silver wire
1 x red oval bead, 10 mm x
  6 mm
Round- and flat-nose pliers
Wire cutters
Ring mandrel or cylindrical
  dowel
Hammer

This ring will fit most finger sizes, as it has a front opening. It is very decorative, but if you would prefer a plainer look, make it with fewer spirals and without the bead. Alternatively, add a bead to every tendril and twist the spiral ends in different directions for a complete design transformation!

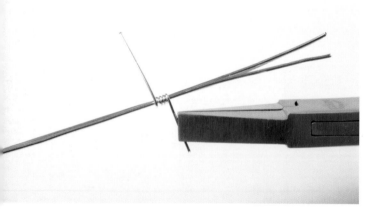

1 Cut three 5-in. (12.5-cm) lengths of 20-gauge (0.8 mm) silver wire and straighten them so that they are parallel to each other. Cut two 2½-in. (6-cm) lengths of 24-gauge (0.6 mm) silver wire. Hold the three thicker wires together, making sure they sit in a line, one above the other. Take one piece of the thinner wire and use it to bind the thicker wires together about 1½ in. (4 cm) from one end.

2 Repeat on the other side. Squeeze the ends of the wrapped wires with your flat-nose pliers to tighten them against the thicker wires.

RIGHT
This very distinctive, dressy ring design looks stunning with any color of focal bead—or, as the alternative designs in the background show, it can be made with more beads or with none at all!

Lover's ring

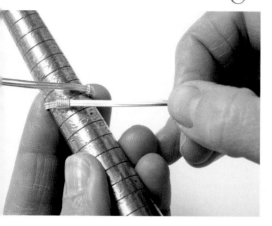

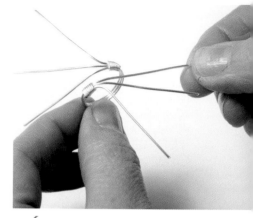

3 Mold the wrapped wires around your ring mandrel to shape them into a circular ring shank, overlapping the ends, one above the other. If you do not have a ring mandrel, use a piece of wooden dowel or narrow curtain pole.

4 Using your fingers, separate the three wires on each side and spread them out in a fan shape.

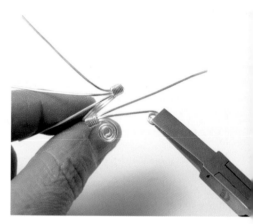

5 On one side, form a small loop at the end of each wire with your round-nose pliers, and then use your flat-nose pliers to create a closed spiral (see page 16).

Variation
Omit the beads and push the outer spirals in toward the center, to cover the wrapped wires on the ring shank.

6 On the other side of the fan, thread the red oval bead onto the first extending wire and push it right up against the wrapped wire frame. Bend the extending wire around the perimeter of the bead.

7 Using your round-nose pliers, make a small loop at the very end of the wire and push it flat against the bead.

8 Repeat Step 5 to create a closed spiral at the end of the remaining two wires.

9 Place the ring back on the mandrel to reshape it. Press the spirals flat against the mandrel and gently stroke hammer the spirals and the back of the ring to work harden them (see page 19).

Variation
Thread all the projecting wires with small beads.

*L*ove eternal necklace

You will need

20-gauge (0.8 mm) and
   24-gauge (0.6 mm) silver wire

20-gauge (0.8 mm) gold wire

1 mm black cord

1 x 8 mm round burgundy bead

2 x 5 mm round purple beads

Round- and flat-nose pliers

Wire cutters

Superglue (optional)

The central motif of this necklace is a heart with a glowing bead, symbolizing love, while the gold rings that link the two sides of the heart together represent the union of two people in a marriage or a relationship. The spirals stand for continuity, or something never ending, and when the cord is attached to both sides of the heart, it is meant to represent "love eternal."

LEFT
This heart pendant is suspended from leather cord and has a casual elegance; for a smarter effect, use silver or gold chain, or a ribbon that blends with your focal bead.

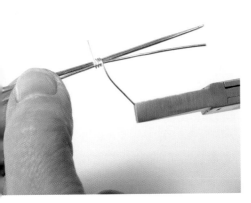

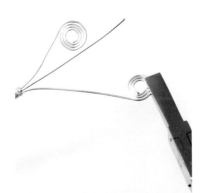

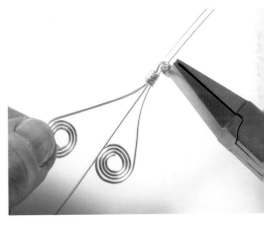

1 Cut two 6-in. (15-cm) lengths of 20-gauge (0.8 mm) silver wire and one 3-in. (7.5-cm) length of 20-gauge (0.8 mm) gold wire. Cut a 2-in. (5-cm) length of 24-gauge (0.6 mm) silver wire and use to bind the three thicker wires together about 1½ in. (4 cm) from the end. Flatten the binding wire with flat-nose pliers and snip off any excess.

2 At the long ends of the two silver wires, make two closed spirals curling in toward each other, approximately ½ in. (1 cm) in diameter (see page 16), with one slightly higher than the other.

3 Form the other end of the gold wire into another closed spiral, ending it right up against the binding wire.

Love eternal necklace

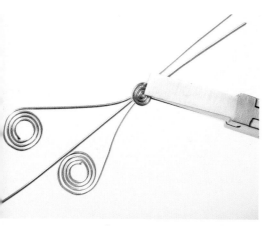

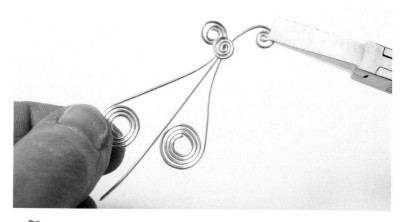

4 Bend the gold spiral over and, using your flat-nose pliers, press it down flat against the binding wire.

5 Pull the two projecting silver wires apart and, using your round-nose pliers, form a circle at each end. Holding the circles firmly in your flat-nose pliers, form a small spiral on each side (see page 16). Make one side slightly shorter than the other to obtain an asymmetrical effect.

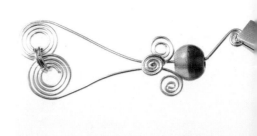

6 Bend the long central gold wire through 180° to the base of the piece.

7 Push the two large silver spirals together so that they touch and form a heart-shaped frame. Make two large jump rings from 20-gauge (0.8 mm) gold wire (see page 16). Loop the jump rings through the holes in the center of the silver spirals to connect the two sides of the frame.

8 Thread the 8 mm burgundy bead onto the projecting gold wire. Curl the end of wire into a closed spiral head pin (see page 15) to secure the bead at the base of the frame.

RIGHT
The central heart-shaped motif, with its pairs of spirals and purple beads, has a pleasing symmetry.

9 Thread the 5 mm purple beads with 20-gauge (0.8 mm) silver wire, forming a wrapped loop at one end and a standard link at the other (see pages 14 and 22).

10 Make two 20-gauge (0.8 mm) wire jump rings (see page 16) to connect one threaded bead to the center of each spiral of the heart frame.

11 Cut the 1 mm cord to the length required. Make two coiled fish-hook clasps (see page 18). Insert each end of the cord into one of the clasps and squeeze the last coil with your flat-nose pliers to secure. (If you wish, put a dab of Superglue inside each coil for added security.)

12 To close the necklace, insert each fish-hook into the wrapped loop at the top of one of the threaded beads.

Chapter 2
Mother's Day

The earliest Mother's Day celebrations can be traced back to the spring festivals of ancient Greece held in honor of Rhea, the mother of the gods. Later, during the 1600s, England commemorated a day called "Mothering Sunday" which was traditionally celebrated on the fourth Sunday of Lent, leading up to Easter. This honored all mothers in England and servants were given the day off to return home and spend time with their families. Today, Mother's Day is a wonderful celebration of motherhood and thanking mothers for all they do.

The thought and time required to make the unique hand-made gifts in this chapter, such as the simple Bow Pin on page 61 or the more complicated Flower Cuff on page 53, will touch any mother's heart.

LEFT
To make a really special Mother's Day gift, use beads in different tones of your mother's favorite color.

Beaded scarf slide

You will need

16-gauge (1.2 mm), 20-gauge
(0.8 mm), and 28-gauge
(0.4 mm) silver wire
1 x 8 mm focal bead
Round- and flat-nose pliers
Wire cutters
Hammer and steel stake

A pretty colored scarf makes a lovely Mother's Day present and this stylish little scarf slide will make the gift even more special. Choose a focal bead that tones in with the colors in the scarf, making sure that the central hole is big enough to be threaded with doubled 20-gauge (0.8 mm) wire.

1 Cut two 5-in. (12.5-cm) lengths of 16-gauge (1.2 mm) silver wire. Using your fingers, twist one wire around the other two or three times about ½ in. (1 cm) from the end. Cut off one of the short ends of wire and flatten the end against the stem with your flat-nose pliers.

2 Form the other short end of wire into a tiny closed spiral (see page 16). Bend the spiral over the wire and, using your flat-nose pliers, squeeze it flat against the wrapped wire to conceal it.

RIGHT
Feed the ends of the scarf under the slanted central bar, so that the focal bead remains visible.

Beaded scarf slide

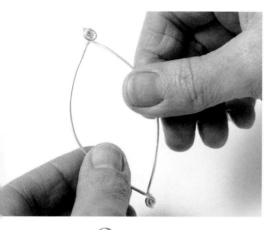

3 Repeat Steps 1 and 2 to secure the other side. Using your fingers, gently pull the sides of the wire frame apart to create an elongated oval shape.

4 Using a hammer on a steel stake, gently stroke hammer the outer frame to work harden it (see page 19), avoiding the spirals.

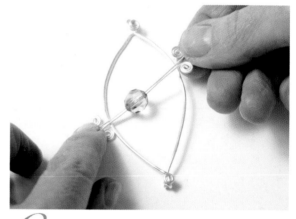

6 The spirals should end just beyond the widest part of the frame; keep checking as you work, to make sure that they're not too big.

5 Cut two 4-in. (10-cm) lengths of 20-gauge (0.8 mm) silver wire, hold them both together in your hand, and thread your focal bead onto the center. At each end of each wire, make a small closed spiral about ¼ in. (5 mm) in diameter, spiraling outward in opposite directions.

LEFT
Check that your focal bead can be threaded with doubled 20-gauge (0.8 mm) wire.

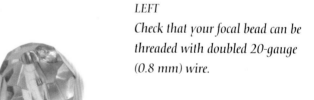

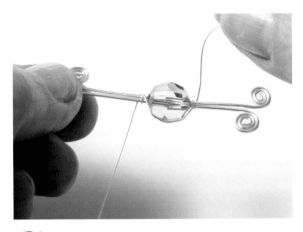

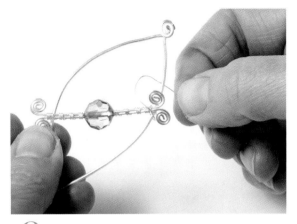

7 Cut a 10–12-in. (20–25-cm) length of 28-gauge (0.4 mm) silver wire. Find the center and wrap it two or three times around the doubled wires, just next to the bead. Take the wire over the back of the bead, then continue wrapping it around the doubled wires in both directions, working right up to the small spirals.

8 Use the ends of the binding wire to attach the beaded bar across the widest point of the frame, angling it slightly on the diagonal.

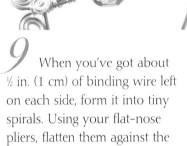

9 When you've got about ½ in. (1 cm) of binding wire left on each side, form it into tiny spirals. Using your flat-nose pliers, flatten them against the bar as extra decoration.

Variation

For a more flamboyant effect, omit Steps 7 and 8, fill the cross bar with beads, and wrap the outer frame in colored wire.

Flower cuff

You will need

12-gauge (2 mm), 20-gauge
   (0.8 mm), and 28-gauge
   (0.4 mm) silver wire
20-gauge (0.8 mm) dark pink
   and light pink wire
Round- and flat-nose pliers
Heavy-duty and standard
   wire cutters
Hammer and steel stake
Mandrel or other cylindrical
   object about 2½ in. (6 cm)
   in diameter

I used two tones of pink for the decorative flowers in this bangle, but you could use a single color (or more!) if you prefer. This design will give you a base pattern from which to make a wide variety of bangles, using beads, colored wire motifs, or even colored buttons. Not only is it a fun piece of jewelry, but it also works well as a napkin ring or as a decorative ring around a glass jar, bottle, or pot.

LEFT
Pink and perky, this colorful little flower bangle is the perfect piece of spring- or summertime jewelry. Why not make several, in different colors, to match different outfits?

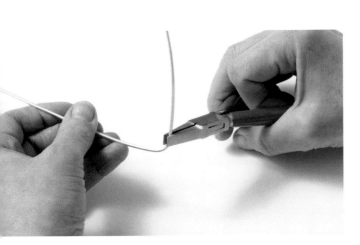

1 Cut a 18-in. (45-cm) length of 12-gauge (2 mm) silver wire. Find the center and, holding it firmly in your flat-nose pliers, bend the wire at an angle of 90°.

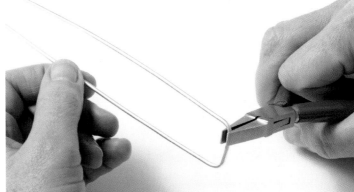

2 Move your pliers about ½ in. (1 cm) along the wire and bend the wire up at 90° again. Using your fingers, straighten both projecting wires so that they run parallel to each other.

Flower cuff

3 At the end of each projecting wire, form an open spiral about ¾ in. (2 cm) in diameter (see page 16). The spirals should curl outward, in opposite directions.

4 Mold the wire around a mandrel or other cylindrical object about 2½ in. (6 cm) in diameter (or large enough to fit your wrist), to shape it into a circular bangle.

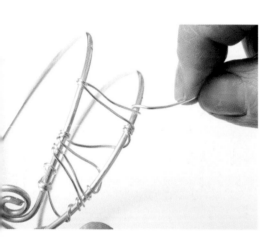

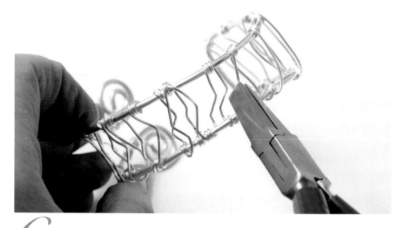

6 Using the tips of your flat-nose pliers, twist and bend the zig-zagged wire into interesting shapes.

5 Cut a 20-in. (50-cm) length of 20-gauge (0.8 mm) silver wire and wrap it around the ends of the spirals to hold the bangle in shape. Continue wrapping the wire along the top and bottom of the frame in an uneven zig-zag pattern, wrapping it two or three times around the frame each time, until you have filled the space. Cut more wire if necessary.

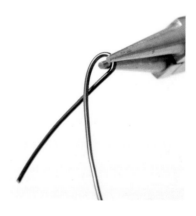

7 Now make colored wire flowers out of 20-gauge (0.8 mm) pink wire. Working directly from the spool, form a loop around the shaft of your round-nose pliers about 1 in. (2.5 cm) from the end of the wire.

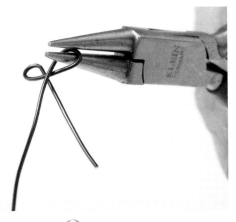

8 Cross the wire over the first loop and make a second loop, opposite the first.

9 Repeat the process, looping the wire around the pliers so that the loops sit opposite each other each time, until you have five or six "petals." Cut the wire off the spool, leaving about 1½ in. (4 cm) extending. Turn the flower shape over and wrap the short end of wire (left from making the first loop in Step 7) around the center of the flower.

10 Press the wrapped wire flat with your flat-nose pliers to secure. Cut off any excess and neaten the ends (see page 21). Using your fingers, adjust the petals so that they are evenly spaced.

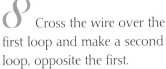

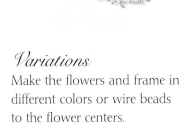

Variations

Make the flowers and frame in different colors or wire beads to the flower centers.

11 Using the tips of your round-nose pliers, curl a hook at the end of the extending wire. Using your flat-nose pliers, squeeze the hook onto the extending wire like a head pin, and then continue coiling the wire around itself to create a tight spiral. Press the spiral onto the center of the flower. Repeat Steps 7–11 to make nine flowers in total–four from dark pink and five from light pink wire.

12 Alternating light and dark pink flowers, bind the flowers to the bangle with 28-gauge (0.4 mm) silver wire, taking the wire under the bent-over central spiral and through the petals until they are firmly attached. Snip off any excess binding wire and neaten the ends (see page 21).

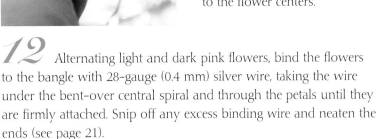

*W*iggly chain

You will need

20-gauge (0.8 mm) silver wire

Approx. 11 x 7–9 mm oval, beige glass beads

Round-, chain-, and flat-nose pliers

Wire cutters

Hammer and steel stake

I included this design in the book, as I made a similar piece some years ago for Mother's Day and my mom still loyally wears it! She says people always remark on it, as it's so unusual and original in style. As you can see from the blue-beaded variation on page 58, it can also be created as a long, continuous necklace, without a clasp. Alternatively, try making it without any beads at all, with a smaller version for a matching bracelet.

RIGHT
The pale beads and fine wire units form a striking, yet understated design that suits all ages.

3 Pull the wire diagonally across the bead back to the first hole, and wrap it around the base of the link to secure. Cut the wire off the spool and neaten up any spiky ends with your chain-nose pliers (see page 21). Repeat Steps 1–3 to thread all the beads. The last bead should have a hammered loop, as this will form the "eye" of the clasp in Step 12.

1 Working from the spool, thread the first bead with 20-gauge (0.8 mm) wire and form a link at one end (see page 14). Place the center of your round-nose pliers at the other end of the bead and bend the wire at a right angle.

2 Pull the wire over the pliers and wrap it around the stem a couple of times to form a loop.

Wiggly chain

4 Working from a spool of 20-gauge (0.8 mm) silver wire, make a link at the end of the wire (see page 14) using your round-nose pliers.

Variation
Mix and match different tones and shapes of beads.

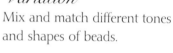

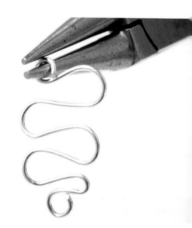

5 Place the tips of your round-nose pliers just under this link and bend the wire around one shaft of the pliers.

6 Move your pliers about ½ in. (1 cm) up the wire and bend the wire around the shaft again, to create a wiggly shape in the wire.

7 Repeat until you have created four more bends. Cut the wire from the spool and, using your round-nose pliers, form a link at the end (see page 14).

8 Push all the "wiggles" together so that they touch one another, then gently hammer the unit on a steel stake to work harden it (see page 19). Repeat Steps 4–8 to make nine more units.

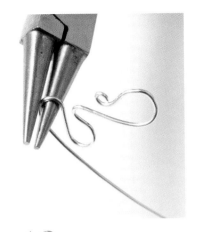

11 Attach the fish-hook clasp to the other end of the necklace.

9 Make jump rings from 20-gauge (0.8 mm) silver wire (see page 16) and connect all the units together, alternating wire units and threaded beads and making sure that the bead with the hammered loop (see Step 3) goes at one end of the chain.

10 Working from a spool of 20-gauge (0.8 mm) silver wire, make a fish-hook clasp (see page 18) and cut the wire off the spool, leaving 2 in. (5 cm) extending. Shape the stem of the fastener by bending it around the shaft of your round-nose pliers, as in Steps 5–7. Gently hammer the fish-hook fastener on a steel stake to work harden it (see page 19).

12 The wrapped loop of the last bead forms the "eye" of the fastener, although the fish-hook fastener can be connected anywhere within the necklace to make it shorter if you prefer.

RIGHT
The semi-translucent glass beads and delicate silver chain units give this necklace a thoroughly feminine feel.

You will need

16-gauge (1.2 mm), 20-gauge
(0.8 mm), and 28-gauge
(0.4 mm) silver wire

Cylindrical mandrel approx.
½ in. (1 cm) in diameter

1 x 8 mm focal bead

Round-, flat-, and chain-nose
pliers

Wire cutters

Hammer and steel stake

Flat needle file

Fine sandpaper

Bow pin

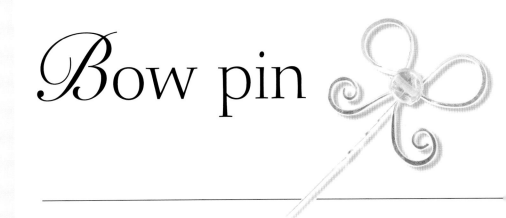

*This simple, yet striking, design looks fantastic worn
on a plain-colored jacket or coat lapel. Alternatively,
make it with a longer pin and turn it into a chic hat pin—
or make the unit using a thinner gauge of wire, thread the
bow frame with beads, and wire it onto a hairgrip as a
decorative hair accessory.*

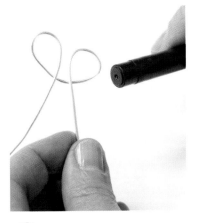

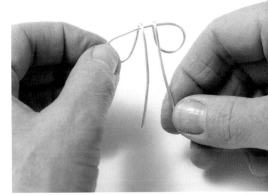

1 Cut 6–8 in. (15–20 cm) of
16-gauge (1.2 mm) silver wire.
Place a mandrel ½ in. (1 cm) in
diameter just by the center of
the wire and bend the wire
around the mandrel to form
a loop, pulling the extending
wire down. (If you haven't got
a mandrel, a round-barrelled
pen will work just as well.)

2 Repeat on the opposite
side of the wire, forming a
second loop.

3 Using your fingers and
flat-nose pliers, pull the
extending wires around the
center wire so that they face
in the opposite direction.

LEFT
*Once you get the hang of making these pretty pins, you'll want to create
them in a variety of colors.*

Bow pin

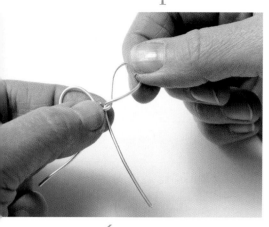

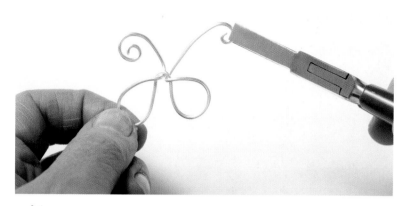

4 Using your fingers, pull up the loops on each side and spend a little time shaping each side of the "bow."

5 Using the tips of your round-nose pliers, form a small loop at one end of each extending wire. Hold this circle firmly in your flat-nose pliers and form an open spiral (see page 16), spiraling outward. Repeat with the other extending wire, again spiraling the wire outward so that the spirals curl in opposite directions.

6 Gently hammer the outer frame to work harden and flatten the metal, making sure you don't hammer any crossed-over wires (see page 19).

7 Cut a 3-in. (7.5-cm) length of 28-gauge (0.4 mm) silver wire. Thread your focal bead onto the center of the wire. Hold the bead in the center of the bow and secure it at the back by wrapping the wire around the bow several times. Neaten the ends (see page 21).

8 To form the pin of the brooch, cut a 3-in. (7.5-cm) length of 20-gauge (0.8 mm) silver wire and form a small, tight spiral at one end (see page 16), leaving approximately 2 in. (5 cm) extending. Using your fingers and flat-nose pliers, straighten out any kinks in the wire.

9 Gently hammer the spiral and the center of the stem to flatten and work harden the pin (see page 19).

10 Using both your flat- and chain-nose pliers, grip the end of the wire and the top spiral very firmly and twist one set of pliers in one direction, four or five times. This will work harden the hammered area and create a non-slip twist on the pin.

11 Rest the pin on a flat surface, such as the edge of your work table, and, using a needle file, file the end of the wire to a point, turning the pin as you work. Finish with fine sandpaper to get rid of any burrs in the metal.

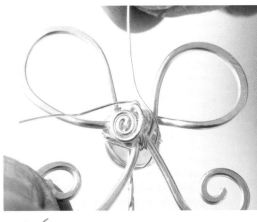

12 Push the pin into the back wires of the bow, behind the bead.

14 Cut a 2-in. (5-cm) length of 28-gauge (0.4 mm) silver wire. Wrap it around the spiral and each side of the bow to bind it firmly in place. Cut off any excess wire and neaten the ends (see page 21).

13 Using your chain-nose pliers, bend the spiral at the end of the pin over. Press it flat against the back of the focal bead.

Chapter 3
Birthdays

A birthday is a day of celebration, and it's especially pleasing to be able to give a unique, hand-made gift to mark the occasion. Use the astrological birthstone chart on page 69 to find the correct gemstone or color of bead for your creation. The symbolism of birthstones seems to have originated in Biblical times; there is a reference in the Book of Exodus to a breastplate of Aaron, naming twelve mounted gemstones, each one representing one of the twelve sons of Israel.

LEFT
This chain bracelet and earrings set can be created using either colored beads or semi-precious chips.

*B*irthstone bracelet

You will need

Turquoise chips
10–12-in. (25–30-cm) length
 of ready-made silver chain
20-gauge (0.8 mm) silver wire
Round- and flat-nose pliers
Wire cutters

To make this bracelet you will need to cut a length of chain in half and then reconnect the ends with jump rings, rather than use a single length of chain as, in my experience, the ends do not taper well. Also, make sure that the links of the ready-made chain are wide enough to thread with 20-gauge (0.8 mm) wire. This design can also make a very original christening gift for a baby girl.

RIGHT
The semi-precious turquoise chip stone used in this bracelet is purported to promote spiritual attunement and well being.

1 Cut two 5–6-in. (12.5–15-cm) lengths of ready-made chain. Make a jump ring from 20-gauge (0.8 mm) silver wire (see page 16) and thread it through one end of each section of chain to join them together.

2 Thread two turquoise chips onto the end of a spool of 20-gauge (0.8 mm) silver wire. Leave about ½ in. (1 cm) protruding on each side of the beads and cut the wire off the spool.

3 Take the chips off the wire. Form a small spiraled head pin at one end of the wire (see page 15). Straighten the other end of the wire if necessary.

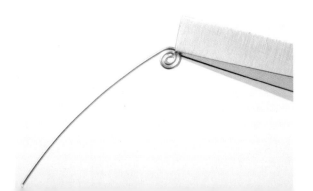

Birthstone bracelet

4 Count three chain links down from the jump ring on one side of the chain and slide the pin into the link from the outside. Rethread the pin with the two turquoise chips and slide it through the third link on the opposite side of the chain.

5 Form a spiraled head pin on the other side to hold the chips in place.

Variations

The bracelet and earrings shown here are made using bugle and seed beads, creating an elegant "ladder" effect.

6 Repeat Steps 2–5 along the length of the bracelet, increasing the chips on each unit to three and then four, or five. Decrease the number of chips at the end of the bracelet. Leave three links of the chain between each beaded unit.

Birthstone chart

Month and zodiac sign	Semi-precious stone	Colour
JANUARY 1–19 Jan. (Capricorn) 20–31 Jan. (Aquarius)	Garnet	Deep red/burgundy
FEBRUARY 1–18 Feb. (Aquarius) 19–28 Feb. (Pisces)	Amethyst	Purple
MARCH 1–20 March (Pisces) 21–31 March (Aries)	Aquamarine	Pale blue
APRIL 1–19 April (Aries) 20–30 April (Taurus)	Diamond/ clear crystal	Clear/colorless
MAY 1–20 May (Taurus) 21–31 May (Gemini)	Emerald	Green
JUNE 1–21 June (Gemini) 22–30 June (Cancer)	Pearl	Cream
JULY 1–22 July (Cancer) 23–31 July (Leo)	Ruby	Bright red
AUGUST 1–22 August (Leo) 23–31 August (Virgo)	Peridot	Pale green
SEPTEMBER 1–22 Sept. (Virgo) 23–30 Sept. (Libra)	Sapphire	Pale blue
OCTOBER 1–23 Oct. (Libra) 24–31 Oct. (Scorpio)	Opal	Variegated/ multi-colored
NOVEMBER 1–21 Nov. (Scorpio) 22–30 Nov. (Sagittarius)	Topaz	Yellow
DECEMBER 1–21 Dec. (Sagittarius) 22–31 Dec. (Capricorn)	Turquoise	Bright blue

7 When the bracelet is full, join the two chains by attaching a jump ring to the chain ends. Position the ring three chain links from the last beaded unit, as shown.

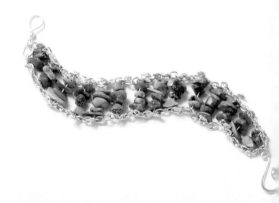

8 Make a fish-hook clasp and eye (see pages 18 and 20) and connect them to the jump rings at each end of the bracelet.

Birthstone necklace

You will need

Amethyst chips

20-gauge (0.8 mm) silver wire

0.5 mm nylon filament

Approx. 40 x 5 mm silver crimp
beads

Round-, chain-, and flat-nose
pliers

Wire cutters

Hammer and steel stake

Tastes in jewelry are highly personal and it is often difficult to know what to create for a special friend's birthday gift. This birthstone necklace is the perfect present. The semi-precious stone amethyst, used in this piece, is associated with February birthdays and the purple color of the stone is symbolic of wisdom and knowledge. Look at the Birthstone Chart on page 69 to find out which stone or bead color you need to buy for your own creation.

3 Make a third loop in the same way, then cut the wire off the spool. Repeat Steps 1–3 to make a second three-loop unit.

LEFT
The natural beauty of the stones gives this necklace and earrings set a classic, timeless quality.

1 Working from a spool of 20-gauge (0.8 mm) silver wire and using your round-nose pliers, curl a complete circle at the end of the wire.

2 Move the pliers next to the first loop and form another loop directly beside it, wrapping the wire around the same section of the pliers so that the loops are roughly the same size.

Birthstone necklace

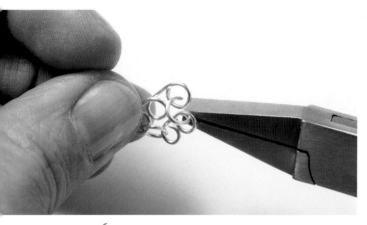

4 Repeat Steps 1 and 2 to make two two-loop units. Make two small jump rings from 20-gauge (0.8 mm) silver wire (see page 16). Using the jump rings, attach each two-loop unit to the base of a three-loop unit, as shown, to form a kind of inverted triangle.

5 Cut three 8-in. (20-cm) lengths of 0.5 mm nylon filament. Thread a silver crimp bead onto the first length. Feed the filament through the first loop of one three-loop unit and double the nylon back onto itself, through the crimp bead, to form a small loop. Squeeze the crimp bead with your chain-nose pliers to secure.

6 Thread the nylon filament with eight amethyst chips, pushing them right up against the crimp bead, and then thread on another crimp bead and squeeze it with your chain-nose pliers to secure. Leave a gap of about ½ in. (1 cm), then secure another crimp bead on the filament. Thread on eight more chips and another crimp bead, as before. Repeat until the filament is full, placing a crimp bead at the start and end of each block of eight chips in order to keep them separate.

7 Attach the second length of filament to the central loop of the same three-loop unit, then fill it with chips, as in Step 6—but this time, make blocks of five amethyst chips. Attach the third length of filament to the remaining loop of the three-loop unit, then fill it with blocks of three amethyst chips. Attach the other ends of the three lengths of filament to the corresponding loops on the second silver unit.

8 To make the chain links, cut 16 2-in. (5-cm) lengths of 20-gauge (0.8 mm) silver wire. Using your round-nose pliers, curl a circle at one end of each wire. Curl another circle at the other end of the wire, facing in toward the first. Hold the circles firmly in your flat-nose pliers and spiral them in toward each other until they meet in the center of the wire.

9 Gently hammer the units on a steel stake to work harden them (see page 19).

10 Make 18 jump rings (see page 16). Starting and ending with a jump ring, connect eight units together to form one side of the chain. Repeat to form the second side.

11 Now attach the chains to the amethyst centerpiece. Make another four jump rings (see page 16). Link one jump ring into each loop of a two-loop unit, then connect them both to the jump ring at the end of each section of chain.

12 Make a fish-hook clasp and eye (see page 18). Attach the clasp to one section of chain and the eye to the other (see page 20).

Variation
I call this a "Positive Energy" necklace, as it combines the energies of different semi-precious stones in one piece. The stones are crimped onto black nylon filament.

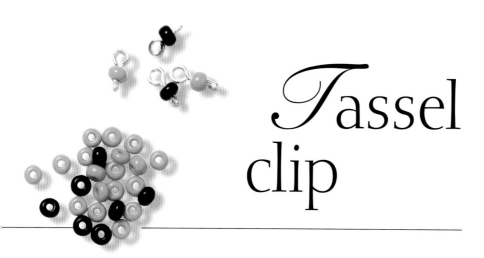

Tassel clip

You will need

25-in. (60-cm) length of ready-made chain

20-gauge (0.8 mm) and 28-gauge (0.4 mm) silver wire

1 x 8 mm turquoise barrel tube bead

1 x 4 mm round silver bead

1 x 1 cm bicone silver bead

5 x size 9/0 turquoise seed beads

5 x size 9/0 black seed beads

Ready-made clip or key-ring finding

Round- and flat-nose pliers

Wire cutters

This fun key ring or handbag charm also looks fabulous suspended from the end of a belt. Chained tassels are simple to make and can be made into dangly earrings, necklace centerpieces, and bracelet charms. You can also adapt them for home furnishings and sew them onto the corners of pillow covers or the ends of curtain tiebacks.

1 Cut ten 2½-in (.6-cm) lengths of ready-made chain.

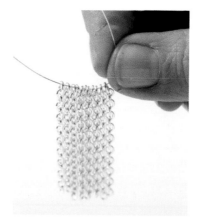

2 Thread the top link of each length of chain onto a 3-in. (7.5-cm) length of 28-gauge (0.4 mm) silver wire.

3 Bring the two ends of the wire together and twist them together to form a short stem about ¼ in. (5 mm) long, above the rows of chain.

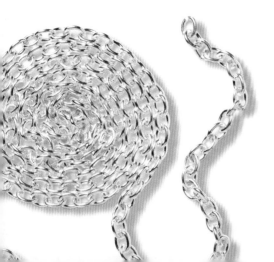

RIGHT
The chained tassel of this clip adds an air of elegance to any purse or bag. Alternatively, just clip it on to the front of a belt loop to personalize a pair of mass-produced jeans.

4 Thread the 8 mm turquoise bead and then the 4 mm silver bead onto the twisted stem. Using your round- and flat-nose pliers, make a wrapped loop (see page 22) with the doubled wire at the top of the bead hole.

5 Thread the 1 cm silver bead onto 20-gauge (0.8 mm) silver wire. Using your round-nose pliers, make a link at each end (see page 14).

6 Connect the tassel to one link of the 1 cm silver bead.

7 Thread five black and five turquoise size 9/0 seed beads individually onto 20-gauge (0.8 mm) silver wire. Form a link at one end and a head pin at the other (see pages 14 and 15).

8 Alternating black and turquoise seed beads, attach one seed bead to each section of the chain tassel by opening the link on the seed bead, looping it through the bottom link of one section of chain, and closing the link again with your flat-nose pliers.

9 Connect the top link of the 1 cm bead to the ready-made key-ring or clip finding.

Variation

The tassel can also be created using a mixture of ribbon and chain.

$\mathcal{F}$lower pin

You will need

24-gauge (0.6 mm) red wire

24-gauge (0.6 mm) green wire

Assorted beads 2–4 mm in size

Lapel pin finding with cap end

Round- and flat-nose pliers

Wire cutters

For a really special hand-made birthday gift, I've devised
this pretty little beaded flower and attached it to a lapel
pin. You could wire the same design onto the top of a gift
box, a hair slide, tiara bands—anything you choose.
You can make the flowers larger by increasing the amount
of wire and chunkier by using a thicker gauge and larger
beads for the center.

1 Working from a spool of
24-gauge (0.6 mm) red wire,
curl a small circle at the end
using the tips of your round-
nose pliers.

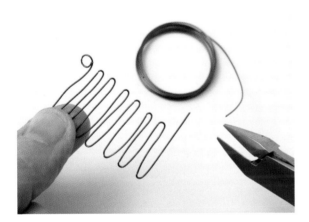

2 Place your round-nose pliers approximately
1 in. (2.5 cm) from the end of the wire and bend
it back down toward the small circle. Repeat,
continuing to bend the wire into a zig-zag shape
until you have about seven zig-zags. Cut the wire
off the spool, leaving about ½ in. (1 cm) extending.

LEFT
*Wear two pins together to make a dramatic corsage
or decoration for a plain-colored hat.*

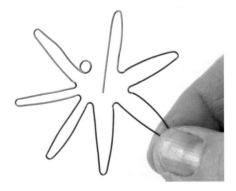

3 Using a combination of your fingers
and flat-nose pliers, pull the zig-zags around
to form a circle.

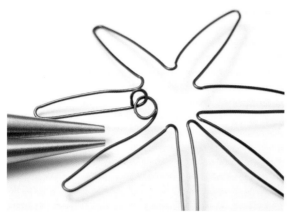

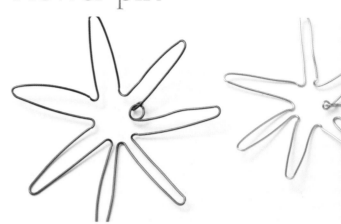

Flower pin

4 Connect the two ends together by pushing the cut end of the wire through the first loop that you made in Step 1 and curling it around the tip of your round-nose pliers to form a second loop.

5 Repeat Steps 1–4 to make a second frame, this time using 24-gauge (0.6 mm) green wire.

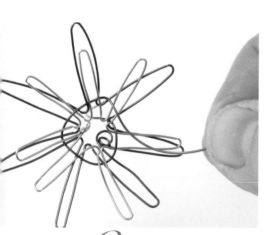

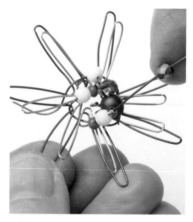

6 Place the green frame on top of the red frame and bind the two centers together with about 12 in. (30 cm) of 24-gauge (0.6 mm) red wire, weaving the wire in between the petals and leaving about 1 in. (2.5 cm) protruding at the back of the flower.

7 Thread the protruding wire with small beads, criss-crossing over the middle of the frames to cover the gap in the center.

8 Pull the end of the wire through to the back. Twist the two protruding wires together to secure.

9 To improve the shape of the petals, place your round-nose pliers inside each red petal and gently open the centers.

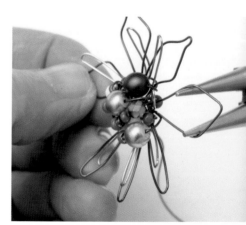

10 Squeeze the end of each red petal with your flat-nose pliers to shape them into points.

11 Using the ends of your round-nose pliers, curl the un-shaped green petals forward, toward the beaded center.

12 Push a lapel pin through the back of the flower and fix it in place by wrapping the twisted wire ends around the top of the pin, so that it cannot slide out. Finally, place the safety cap on the base of the pin.

RIGHT
Not only does this pin look attractive in a hat, but it can also be worn as a brooch in a jacket lapel.

Chapter 4
Weddings

The word "wed" is derived from the ancient Greek word for "pledge"—and that's exactly what a wedding is, in every culture and country in the world. Even though it is a solemn pledge, it is also such a joyous celebration of human existence—the embodiment of two hearts beating as one. I hope that the projects in this chapter, which range from a fun, bridesmaid's wand in place of the traditional posy to the bridal headdress, complete with necklace and earrings, will inspire different design ideas that you can adapt to suit the occasion. You could even incorporate some of the "heart" designs from the Valentine's Day chapter into your wedding pieces.

LEFT
This decorative beaded dragonfly could be placed in the bride's bouquet, or put into a floral centerpiece, to continue the theme throughout the wedding.

Bride's tiara

You will need

20-gauge (0.8 mm) silver wire

28-gauge (0.4 mm) gold wire

Tiara band

Approx. 80 x size 9/0 silver seed beads

Approx. 16 x 4 mm gold-plated beads

Approx. 16 x 6 mm gold-plated beads

Round- and flat-nose pliers

Wire cutters

A stylish tiara is guaranteed to make any bride feel like a princess for her special day. Although this design looks complex, it is actually quite simple to make. I hope it will spark off ideas for a headpiece using beads of your choice to go with the bride's dress or the overall color scheme of the wedding. Freshwater pearls and crystal beads, or ivory and salmon pearls, make stunning combinations.

RIGHT
This tiara can be made using any color of bead. For a bolder crown, form higher peaks and thread with larger beads.

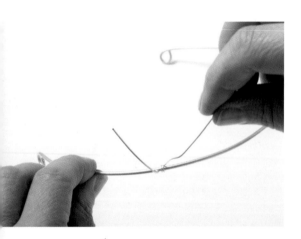

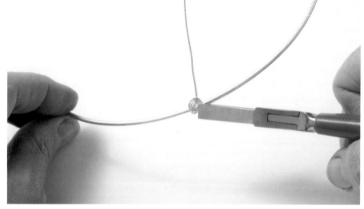

1 Cut approximately 24–30 in. (60–75 cm) of 20-gauge (0.8 mm) silver wire. Leaving about 1 in. (2.5 cm) of wire extending, and starting about 4 in. (10 cm) in from the end of the tiara frame, wrap the wire two or three times tightly around the frame to secure.

2 Form a small, closed spiral at the end of the extending wire (see page 16). Flatten the spiral against the frame to hide the wrapped wire underneath, and press it down with your flat-nose pliers.

Bride's tiara

Variations

Both variations show how easily you can adapt this project. The tiara on the left has red and silver beads, while the pearl and crystal tiara has been wired with extra stalks of wire threaded with more pearl beads, secured with Superglue at the tips.

3 Thread on a 6 mm gold bead, then bend the wire around the tips of your round-nose pliers to form a peak.

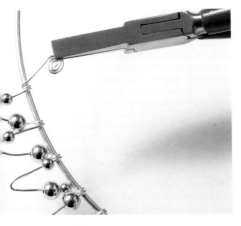

4 Thread on a 4 mm gold bead and secure by wrapping the wire once around the frame. Continue, adding 6 mm and 4 mm gold beads to each peak as you work. The peaks do not have to be symmetrical.

5 When you are about 1½ in. (4 cm) from the end of the frame, wrap the wire a couple of times around the frame to secure. Form a small, closed spiral, as in Step 2, and flatten it against the wrapped wires to conceal them.

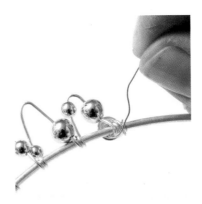

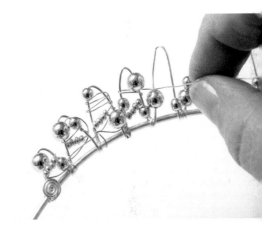

6 Cut about 24 in. (60 cm) of 28-gauge (0.4 mm) gold wire and wrap it underneath one of the side spirals to secure.

7 Continue wrapping this thinner gold wire around the framework, threading it randomly with silver seed beads. If you run out of wire, just cut some more and continue wrapping.

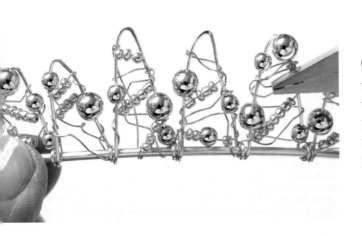

8 Continue filling the wiggly peaks with wrapped wire and beads until you are satisfied with the effect. Spend a little time readjusting your tiara framework using your fingers and flat-nose pliers and make sure that the wire peaks are centered on the tiara frame.

You will need

- 20-gauge (0.8 mm) gold wire
- 6 x 5 mm pearls
- 1 x 1 cm pearl
- 24 x size 9/0 white pearl seed beads
- 8 x size 9/0 gold seed beads
- Round- and flat-nose pliers
- Wire cutters
- Hammer and steel stake

*P*early necklace

This design of beautiful pearl beads on gold wire harks back to the style of Victorian jewelry at the turn of the last century and would look stunning against an ivory-colored wedding dress. For evening wear, make it using clear crystals or colored Swarovski beads.

1 To make the central hanger of the necklace, cut a 2-in. (5-cm) length of 20-gauge (0.8 mm) gold wire. Find the center of the wire with your round-nose pliers and wrap the wires around one of the circular shafts, crossing the wires over in opposite directions to form a central loop.

LEFT
Gold and pearls–a classic combination. To make matching earrings, follow Step 8 of the necklace, add seed beads to the wire stems and connect the threaded beads onto ready-made ear wires.

2 Using your round-nose pliers, create a small link at each end of the wire, curling outward in opposite directions (see page 14).

Pearly necklace

3 Hammer the unit on a steel stake to work harden it, taking care not to touch the crossed-over wires as this will weaken them.

4 To make the chain, cut 24 1½-in. (4-cm) lengths of 20-gauge (0.8 mm) gold wire. Thread a pearl seed bead onto each length and form a beaded S-link.

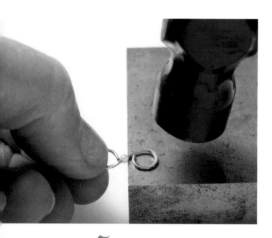

5 Stroke hammer the ends of each unit on a steel stake (see page 19), making sure you do not hammer the beads.

6 Make 26 jump rings (see page 16). Starting and ending with a jump ring, connect the S-links together in two sections of 12 units each.

7 Attach one end of each section of chain to the central hanger that you made in Steps 1–3.

8 Cut six 1-in. (2.5-cm) lengths of 20-gauge (0.8 mm) gold wire and form a head pin at one end of each length. Thread each wire with a gold seed bead, followed by a 5 mm pearl bead. Using your round-nose pliers, make a link at the opposite end of the wire (see page 14), leaving a little stem just under ¼ in. (5 mm) long.

9 Cut a 1½-in. (4-cm) length of 20-gauge (0.8 mm) gold wire and form a head pin at one end. Thread on one gold seed bead, the 1 cm pearl and another gold seed bead. Form a link at the other end of the wire (see page 14).

10 Connect the large pearl to the central loop of the hanger, with three of the smaller, 5 mm pearls on each side, linked into the jump rings in between the S-links.

Variation
This variation has just one focal bead, with the "hanger" frame threaded with pearl seed beads.

11 To complete the necklace, make an S-link clasp (see page 20), and attach it to one end of the necklace. You do not need to make a separate eye for the fastener, as the S-link clasp is simply hooked into any beaded S-link, so the length of the necklace can be adjusted to suit the wearer.

*B*ridal hair grip

You will need

28-gauge (0.4 mm) and
 20-gauge (0.8 mm) gold wire
Pearl, gold bugle, and crystal
 beads, 2–8 mm in diameter
1 x 1 cm pearl feature bead
Masking tape
Nylon filament
Gold-colored crimp beads
Hair grip
Round- and flat-nose pliers
Wire cutters

This bridal hair grip is stylish and decorative and can be clipped onto the side or the back of the head. It can be made in any color of wire, with beads to match the wedding colors or bouquet. Alternatively, make it with brightly colored beads as a decorative hair ornament for a smart engagement party and attach it to the side of a hairband.

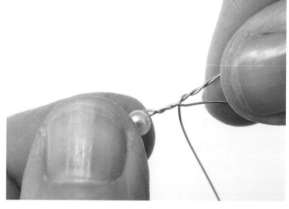

1 Cut four 16-in. (40-cm) lengths of 28-gauge (0.4 mm) gold-plated wire. Place your round-nose pliers in the center of each piece and bend it in half. Where the wires cross, twist them around one another to form a loop. Continue twisting until you have created a twist about 1 in. (2.5 cm) long.

2 Separate the untwisted wires and thread one with a pearl bead. Bring the wire around the top of the bead and back toward the bead hole, holding it in place. Twist the wire three or four times around the second wire to make a short stem.

RIGHT

This stylish hair grip provides instant glamor. Pin it at the back of the head to hide the comb on the veil.

Bridal hair grip

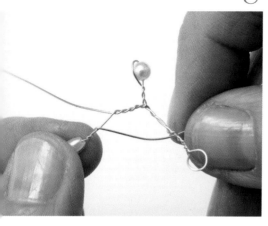

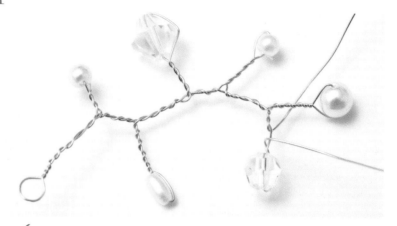

3 Thread another bead onto the other wire and repeat Step 2, creating another beaded stem as before.

4 Continue threading the beads and twisting the wires together until you have created a complete beaded "branch" with six or seven stems and a mixture of beads. Repeat Steps 1–4 to bead all four pieces of wire that you cut in Step 1.

5 Using your flat-nose pliers, squeeze the end loop of each "branch" and twist the wires around to obtain fully twisted stems on all four beaded branches.

LEFT
The beaded tendrils float from the central pearl and add movement and sparkle when worn.

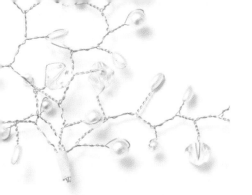

6 Bunch the branches together and tape the stalks together with masking tape. Spend a little time rearranging and shaping the wires into an attractive shape. Where the branches overlap, twist the beads over one another to connect them together, providing the piece with more stability.

7 Using your round-nose pliers, make a ¼-in. (5-mm) coil of 20-gauge (0.8 mm) gold wire, leaving about 1 in. (2.5 cm) of wire extending at one end.

8 Thread the 1 cm pearl feature bead onto this wire. Form a small spiral head pin at the end of the wire (see page 15).

9 Place the taped stems in the coil of wire. Using your flat-nose pliers, squeeze the last ring of the coil tightly against the stems to secure.

10 Cut a 3-in. (7.5-cm) length of 28-gauge (0.4 mm) gold-plated wire and wrap it around the top end of the hair grip and the top of the coil to attach the hair grip to the beaded branches.

11 Cut four 6–8-in. (15–20-cm) lengths of nylon filament. Wrap the center of each filament around the pearl feature bead and the hair grip, and secure by feeding both ends through a gold-colored crimp bead. Push the crimp bead up as far as it will go.

12 Thread the lengths of filament with small pearl, gold bugle, and crystal beads and crimp them in place to create beaded tendrils.

$\mathcal{B}$ridesmaid's necklace

You will need

20-gauge (0.8 mm) and
  28-gauge (0.4 mm) silver wire

Approx. 35 x size 9/0 pearl seed
  beads

1 x 8 mm faded pink faceted bead

4 x 6 mm faded pink faceted beads

12-in. (30-cm) length of ready-
  made chain

Round- and flat-nose pliers

Wire cutters

The beauty of making necklaces for the flower girls and bridesmaids is that they can be given as gifts on the day of the wedding, as a memento of a very special occasion. Pick colors from the dresses or flower posies to provide color continuity.

LEFT

This simple, yet decorative necklace and earrings set, with its tiny seed pearls and transparent beads, also looks fabulous for evening wear.

1 Thread your 8 mm focal bead onto a spool of 20-gauge (0.8 mm) silver wire. Using your round-nose pliers, form a small link about ½ in. (1 cm) from the end of the wire (see page 14).

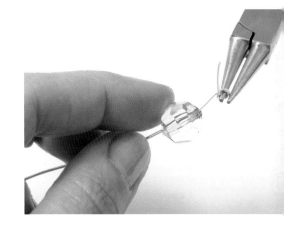

2 Curl the very tip of the wire around in the opposite direction to form a figure-eight.

3 Cut the wire off the spool, leaving about ½ in. (1 cm) projecting beyond the bead. Form this projecting end into a link (see page 14).

Bridesmaid's necklace

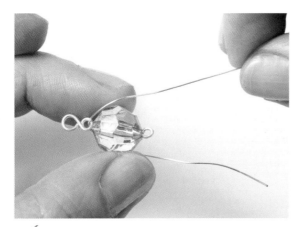

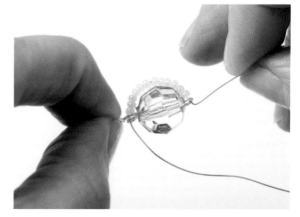

4 Thread 28-gauge (0.4 mm) silver wire through the bottom link of the figure-eight, and bring the wire around the circumference of the bead to encircle it, leaving approximately 1½ in. (4 cm) of wire projecting at each end of the bead.

5 Thread one side of the wire encircling the bead with pearl seed beads, then feed the wire through the bottom link of the focal bead. Feed more seed pearl beads onto the other side of the same wire, until the bead is fully framed.

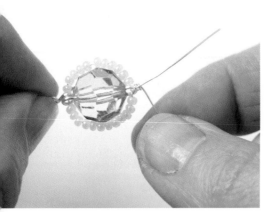

6 Thread one of the wires through one side of the top link and the other one through the opposite side. Where they meet, twist the two wires together to secure. Wrap one wire two or three times around the other and cut off any excess above the wrapped wire, leaving only one projecting wire. Neaten the ends (see page 21) and, using your fingers, mold the beaded frame around the focal bead.

7 Thread one more pearl seed bead onto the projecting stem, and make a wrapped loop (see page 22).

8 Thread three 6 mm beads onto 28-guage (0.4 mm) silver wire, with a pearl seed bead above and below. Form a link and a head pin on one bead, and a link at both ends of the other two beads (see pages 14 and 15).

Variation

This gold-wire variation with matching earrings omits the pendant drop bead. Connect a loop of gold chain on each side of the centerpiece to frame the beads on either side.

9 Attach the first 6 mm bead (the one with the head pin) to the focal bead by opening the link at the top, looping it through the link at the base of the focal bead, and reclosing the link with your flat-nose pliers.

10 Make a large jump ring from 20-gauge (0.8 mm) silver wire (see page 16). Open it, and feed it through the link at the top of the focal bead and the top links on the remaining two 6 mm beads, as shown. Close the jump ring with your flat-nose pliers.

11 Cut two 6-in. (15-cm) lengths of ready-made chain. (The links must be large enough to take 20-gauge/0.8 mm wire.) Attach one end of each section to the top of one of the 6 mm beads by opening the link, feeding it through the chain, and closing the link with your flat-nose pliers.

12 Make a fish-hook clasp (see page 18) and a beaded eye (see page 22) and attach to the other ends of the sections of chain.

Bridesmaid's wand

You will need

12-gauge (2 mm) pink wire

20-gauge (0.8 mm) wire in two
   tones of pink

24-gauge (0.6 mm) fuchsia pink
   wire

100 x size 9/0 pink seed beads

90 x size 9/0 pearl seed beads

Round- and flat-nose pliers

Wire cutters

Hammer and steel stake

Mandrel or cylindrical dowel
   ½ in. (1 cm) in diameter

The beauty of a wand, as opposed to a posy of fresh flowers, is that the bridesmaid can keep and treasure it as a reminder of a very special day. Use wire and beads in a color that matches the bridesmaids' dresses. Other beaded motifs—perhaps butterflies, hearts or flowers—can be suspended from the top hooks in place of the dragonfly shown here.

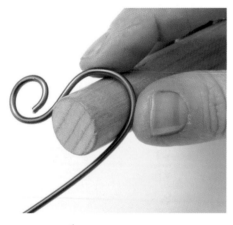

1 Cut a 14–16-in. (35–40-cm) length of 12-gauge (2 mm) pink wire for the wand stem. Using your round-nose pliers, form a loop at one end. Place the mandrel just below the loop and bend the wire about halfway around it in the opposite direction to form a shape like a shepherd's crook.

2 Using your round- and flat-nose pliers, form an open spiral at the other end of the wire (see page 16). Hammer the top loop and the base spiral on a steel stake to work harden the wire (see page 19).

RIGHT
These pretty wands are the perfect accessory for very young flower girls as they are light and easy to carry.

3 To make the dragonfly, cut a 6-in. (15-cm) length of the first tone of 20-gauge (0.8 mm) pink wire. Using your round-nose pliers, form a small closed spiral at one end (see page 16). Cut a 6½-in. (16-cm) length of the second tone of 20-gauge (0.8 mm) pink wire and wrap it around the top of the spiral to secure. Continue wrapping it around the stem wire for just over 1 in. (2.5 cm).

Bridesmaid's wand

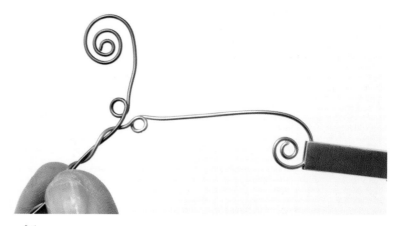

4 Using the tips of your round-nose pliers, curl a small loop, curling outward, in each wire, just below the end of the twist. Straighten and pull the loops up to make the dragonfly's "eyes."

5 Using your round-nose pliers, curl a small circle at the end of each projecting wire. Hold the circle tightly in your flat-nose pliers and form open spirals, curling in opposite directions, for the dragonfly's "antennae."

6 Cut a 20-in. (50-cm) length of 24-gauge (0.6 mm) fuchsia pink wire. Wrap it two or three times around the stem, leaving the same amount of wire extending on each side of the dragonfly's body. Thread 40 pink seed beads onto one end and bend it into a loop to make the first wing. Wrap the wire two or three times around the dragonfly's body, but do not cut off the excess.

7 Thread the remainder of the same wire with 40 pink seed beads and secure as before, to form a second wing on the other side of the dragonfly's body. Do not cut off the excess wire.

8 Repeat Steps 9 and 10, threading the other extending wire with pearl seed beads to form a second row of dragonfly wings.

9 Pull one of the projecting wires up into the center and wrap it around the body, just under the eyes, leaving approximately 1 in. (2.5 cm) extending.

10 Using your round-nose pliers, form a link by curling the end of the wire around the circular shaft until it sits between the eyes and the antennae.

11 Thread the remaining projecting wire with seed beads, alternating two pink beads with one pearl, until you are left with just 1 in. (2.5 cm) of wire extending. At the end of the wire form a small spiral (see page 16), leaving a ¼-in. (5-mm) gap between the spiral and the beads. Hold the spiral in your fingers and curl the beaded wire into a spiral, then flatten it against the dragonfly's body with your fingers.

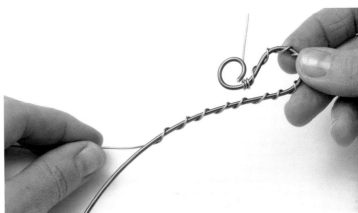

12 Decorate the stem of the wand by wrapping it with 20-gauge (0.8 mm) pale pink wire or ribbon.

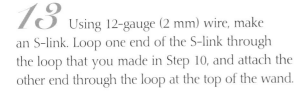

13 Using 12-gauge (2 mm) wire, make an S-link. Loop one end of the S-link through the loop that you made in Step 10, and attach the other end through the loop at the top of the wand.

Chapter 5
Christmas

Today, the religious meaning of Christmas is slowly being overtaken by a time of overspending and self-indulgence and it is good to be able to return to the past, when life was simpler and gifts were hand crafted. The jewelry projects in this chapter provide you with wonderful gift ideas that you can also adapt as decorations for your home.

LEFT
Red and green is a classic color combination for Christmas projects. This matching necklace and earring set was inspired by the conical shape of a stylized Christmas tree (see page 124).

Christmas star pendant

You will need

- 20-gauge (0.8 mm) and 28-gauge (0.4 mm) silver wire
- 54 x size 9/0 multi-colored seed beads
- 1 x 1 cm focal bead
- 6 x 4 mm silver beads
- Round- and flat-nose pliers
- Wire cutters
- Mandrel, about ½ in. (1 cm) in diameter
- Hammer and steel stake (optional)
- Superglue (optional)

It's fun to wear festive jewelry for the Christmas party season—and this star pendant will get everyone talking! If you feel the multicolored version shown here looks too flashy, you could use subtle silver beads and sparkling crystals instead. You can also increase the diameter of the central circle and omit the focal bead, so that the inner ring can be pushed over a candle to create a stunning table decoration.

LEFT
These festive-looking pendants will also add sparkle and color to your Christmas tree.

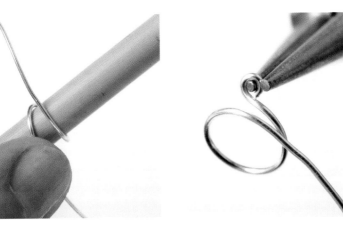

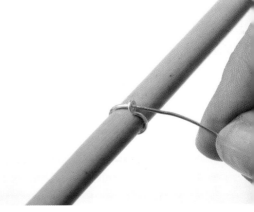

1 Working from a spool of 20-gauge (0.8 mm) silver wire, wrap the wire once around the mandrel to form a complete circle. (If you haven't got a mandrel, use a round-barrelled pen.) Cut the wire off the spool, leaving a stem about 1 in. (2.5 cm) long.

2 Use the very tips of your round-nose pliers, form a little loop at the start of the circle of wire. Using your flat-nose pliers, twist the loop so that it sits at 90° to the rest of the circle.

3 Pull the circle open and thread the long, projecting end of the wire through the loop. Place the circle back onto the mandrel to reshape it.

Christmas star pendant

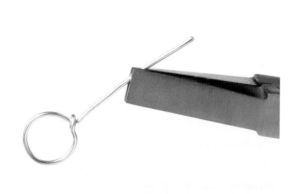

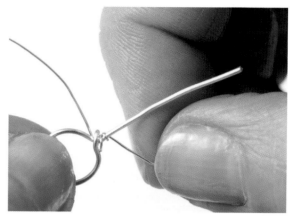

4 Using your flat-nose pliers, bend the extended wire up, so that it projects out from the top of the small loop. If you wish, you can gently tap the circular frame with a hammer on a steel stake to work harden it.

5 Cut a 12-in. (30-cm) length of 28-gauge (0.4 mm) silver wire. Wrap one end two or three times around the stem to secure it.

6 Thread five colored seed beads onto the wire. Place your flat-nose pliers just past the last bead and bend the wire around the pliers.

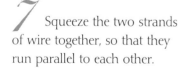

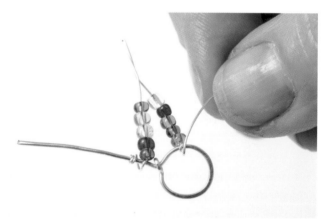

7 Squeeze the two strands of wire together, so that they run parallel to each other.

8 Pull the projecting wire down toward the circle and thread on five more seed beads before wrapping the wire around the circular frame. You have now made the first point of the star.

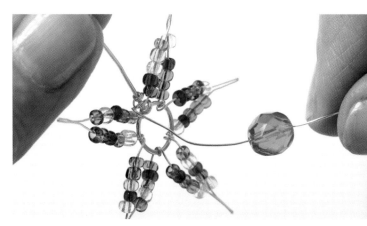

9 Repeat Steps 6–8 to form four more points around the circle. When you reach the end, wrap the fine wire around the extending stem to secure it, but do not cut off the excess.

10 Thread a 1 cm focal bead onto the thin wire, push it into the center of the circle, and secure the wire by wrapping it around the frame. Snip off any excess, and neaten the ends (see page 21).

12 Thread four seed beads followed by a 4 mm silver bead onto the stem. Using your round-nose pliers, form a link at the top of the bead (see page 14). The pendant is now ready to suspend from a chain, ribbon, or cord of your choice.

11 Thread a silver 4 mm bead onto the doubled wires at each point of the star. Form a tiny head pin (see page 15) on the points to prevent the beads from slipping off. If you wish, you can put a dab of Superglue by the bead and head pin for extra security.

Variation

The star earrings are made in exactly the same way as the pendant, but instead of using colored seed beads, purple bugle and 4 mm round silver beads have been substituted.

Holly-leaf necklace

This simple design can be increased or decreased in scale to suit your style. Have fun varying the color of the beads and wire for a totally different impression. The holly motif can also be attached to satin ribbons and tied around napkins for an original festive table setting, or suspended on clear fishing line and hung in the window to catch the frosty sparkle of Yuletide!

RIGHT
The crystal and silver of this piece have a festive, Christmassy feel. Try using copper wire and threading the center with green beads and you will suddenly find the design metamorphoses into an autumnal oak leaf.

1 Working from a spool of 20-gauge (0.8 mm) wire, place the tips of your round-nose pliers 1 in. (2.5 cm) from the end and bend the wire at 90°.

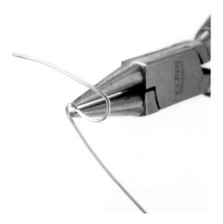

2 Place the widest part of your round-nose pliers just next to the bend in the wire and curve it around to form a U-shape.

3 Repeat Steps 1 and 2 to make three more U-shapes, which will eventually form one side of the leaf.

4 Make a fourth U-shape, slightly longer and more elongated than the previous ones; this will be the tip of the leaf.

Holly-leaf necklace

 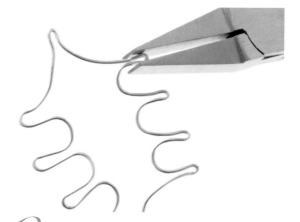

5 Bring the wire up and make four more U-shapes to form the opposite side of the leaf. Bring the wires together and wrap the cut end around the stem to secure. Cut the wire off the spool, leaving about 1 in. (2.5 cm) extending.

6 Using your flat-nose pliers, squeeze the tip of each U-shaped curve to create a slightly more spiky appearance, but keep a slightly open channel at the tip of the leaf. Adjust the shape with your fingertips if necessary.

7 Gently hammer the outer frame of the leaf on a steel stake to work harden it, making sure you do not touch the wrapped wires of the stem.

Variation
Make matching earrings by following Steps 1–10 of the necklace and suspending the units from ready-made ear wires.

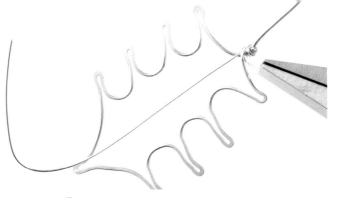

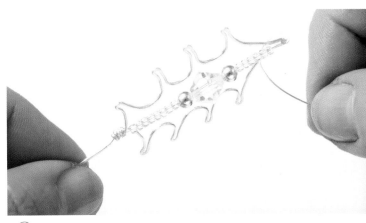

8 Cut a piece of 28-gauge (0.4 mm) silver wire about 1½ in. (4 cm) longer than the leaf. Wrap one end around the stem of the leaf to secure, and pull the wire down the center of the leaf frame.

9 Thread this fine wire with six crystal seed beads, a 4 mm silver bead, a 7 mm bicone crystal, another silver bead, and finally six more crystal seed beads. Secure the wire at the tip end of the leaf in the channel or gap that was left in Step 6. Snip off any excess and neaten the ends (see page 21).

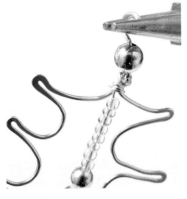

10 Thread a 5 mm silver bead onto the stem and create a link at the other end of the bead hole using your round-nose pliers (see page 14).

11 Cut 20 2-in. (5-cm) lengths of 20-gauge (0.8 mm) silver wire. Form each one into an S-link.

12 Make 21 jump rings from 20-gauge (0.8 mm) silver wire (see page 16). Starting and ending with a jump ring, connect the S-links together in a chain.

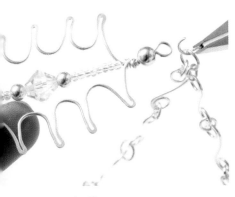

13 Suspend the holly leaf from the central jump ring of the chain.

14 Make an S-link fastener with a wrapped loop (see page 20) and attach it to the ends of the chain.

Beaded bauble pendant

You can make this beaded bauble as delicate or as chunky as you like, depending on the quantity and size of beads you use. The purple bugle beads and clear and white glass beads shown here have an icy, wintry flavour, but a mix of vibrant colors would give it more of a party feel. It's a great design for using up beads left over from other projects. It looks fabulous as a necklace worn with jeans and a sweater—and when it's not being worn, you can hang it on your Christmas tree! We suspended it from a length of ready-made chain, but you could use cord, ribbon, or leather if you prefer.

You will need

- 20-gauge (0.8 mm) and 24-gauge (0.6 mm) silver wire
- 0.5 mm clear nylon filament/fishing line
- 2 x 1 mm silver-colored crimp beads
- Approx. 14 assorted beads in clear and white glass, varying in size from 6 mm to 8 mm
- Approx. 40 x 5 mm bugle beads
- 16-in. (40-cm) length of ready-made silver chain
- Round- and flat-nose pliers
- Wire cutters

LEFT
The cool, frost-like colors of this necklace give it a very wintry feel.

1 Begin by threading your beads with wire. Thread the bugle beads two or three at a time onto 24-gauge (0.6 mm) silver wire and form a doubled head pin at one end (see page 15). Thread the larger beads individually onto 20-gauge (0.8 mm) silver wire.

2 Using your round-nose pliers, form a link at the other end of every bead (see page 14).

Beaded bauble pendant

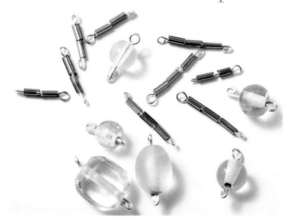

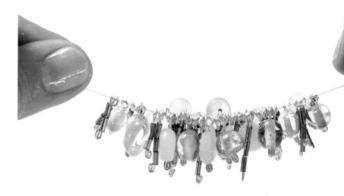

3 Carry on threading the beads, until you have created about 24 pieces in all.

4 Cut a 3–4-in. (7–10-cm) length of clear nylon filament and thread your beads onto this. It doesn't matter in which order you thread the beads, but aim for a fairly even distribution of the purple bugle beads.

5 Pull both ends of the nylon filament together and thread on a silver crimp bead. Push the crimp bead right up to the bundle of threaded beads to form the "bauble" shape. Squeeze the crimp bead tightly with your flat-nose pliers to secure.

6 Using your round-nose pliers, make a coil of 20-gauge (0.8 mm) silver wire about ¼ in. (5 mm) long (see page 23).

7 Thread the coil onto the two strands of nylon filament.

8 Cut off one of the filaments just above the coil. (Be very careful not to cut through both filaments!)

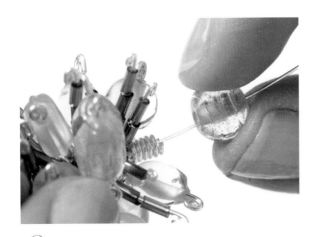

9 Thread a large, clear bead onto the one remaining filament.

10 Slide on one crimp bead and push it right up to the clear bead. Push the end of the filament all the way back through the crimp bead to form a loop. Squeeze the crimp bead with your flat-nose pliers to secure, then cut off any excess filament.

11 Thread ready-made chain or ribbon through the loop to complete the pendant.

Variation

Made from an eclectic mix of chunky beads in varying shades of green, this variation makes a bold statement.

$\mathcal{C}$hristmas wreath necklace

RIGHT
The circular "wreath" of wire is very easy to make. Increase the size to make a napkin ring.

I based this design on the decorated wreaths that are so popular at Christmas time. You could use colored beads and wires if you prefer, but the silver and red color combination has a timeless quality that means you can wear it all year round. Matching earrings can be made as simple, wire wreaths without the central bead; "hoop" earrings are always popular.

You will need

- 20-gauge (0.8 mm) silver wire
- 28-gauge (0.4 mm) silver wire
- 1 x 1 cm red focal bead
- 1 x 7 mm red barrel bead
- Approx. 28 in. (70 cm) ready-made chain
- 36 in. (90 cm) red suede cord
- Round- and flat-nose pliers
- Wire cutters
- Cylindrical mandrel approx. ¾ in. (2 cm) in diameter
- Hammer and steel stake
- Superglue (optional)

1 Working from a spool of 20-gauge (0.8 mm) silver wire, wrap the wire about three times around a cylindrical mandrel about ¾ in. (2 cm) in diameter. Cut the wire from the spool, leaving about 12 in. (30 cm) projecting.

2 Wrap the shorter cut end of the wire around the loops of wire to secure them as one neat circle. Neaten the ends (see page 21).

3 Wrap the long projecting wire around the circular frame, leaving one wrap very loose to provide a gap from which you can suspend the tassel in Step 10.

4 When all the wire has been used up, neaten the ends (see page 21). Place the unit on a steel stake and hammer both sides to flatten and work harden the wire.

5 Above left: Working from the spool, thread a 1 cm red focal bead onto 20-gauge (0.8 mm) silver wire and form a link at the very end of the wire (see page 14). Above right: Push the bead up against the link. About ¼ in. (5 mm) beyond the bead, bend the wire at right angles and wrap it around the shaft of your round-nose pliers to form a second loop. Wrap the wire two or three times around the stem, just under the loop.

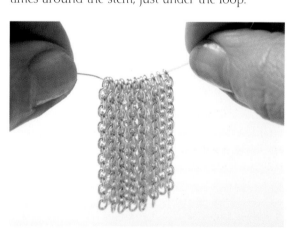

Variations

Thread the wreath with seed beads and suspend a bow in the center. Alternatively, use the wreath as a frame for a handmade bead.

6 Bring the wire across the bead and wrap it around the link at the top. Cut the wire off the spool and neaten the ends (see page 21).

7 Cut 12–14 pieces of ready-made chain, 1½–2 in. (4–5 cm) long. Cut a 3-in. (7.5-cm) length of 28-gauge (0.4 mm) silver wire and thread the last link of each section of chain onto it.

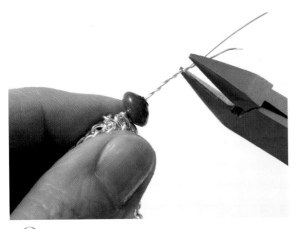

8 Bring the ends of the thinner wire together and twist them around each other several times, close to the sections of chain, to form a tassel. The twisted section should be about ¾ in. (2 cm) long. Thread the small red bead onto the twisted stem and push it up against the tassel. Cut the wire, leaving about ½ in. (1 cm) of stem.

9 Using your round-nose pliers, form the twisted stem into a link (see page 14). Loop the link through the wrapped loop of the red focal bead, and close it with your flat-nose pliers.

10 Using your flat-nose pliers, open the link at the other end of the bead. Feed the link through the loose wrap in the wreath that you formed in Step 3, then close it again with your flat-nose pliers to attach the tassel to the wreath.

11 Cut two 18-in. (45-cm) lengths of red suede cord. Fold one in half to form a loop, and feed the loop under the wreath from the back. Feed the loose ends through the loop and pull to tighten the cord around the wreath. Repeat on the other side of the wreath.

12 Make a coiled fish-hook clasp and "eye" from 20-gauge (0.8 mm) silver wire (see page 18), making sure that the coil is big enough to take a doubled length of suede cord. Feed the clasp onto one end of the suede and the "eye" onto the other, and squeeze the last ring of each coil with your flat-nose pliers to secure. If you wish, you can place a small dab of Superglue on the ends of the suede for added security.

Christmas tree earrings

These earrings are based on the triangular shape of a stylized Christmas tree. This is a quick and fun idea to make as a gift for friends and family. For the perfect pair of celebratory earrings, make it with colored green wire for the outer coil and a line of red, sparkling crystal beads down the center.

1 Using your round- and flat-nose pliers and working from a spool of 20-gauge (0.8 mm) silver wire, form a closed spiral at least ½ in. (1 cm) in diameter. Cut the wire off the spool, leaving about 1 in. (2.5 cm) extending. If you wish, you can gently hammer the spiral on a steel stake to work harden it.

2 Push your round-nose pliers into the center of the spiral and pull the wire down with your fingers to form an evenly spaced, tapered coil.

3 Thread a length of nylon filament through the center of the coil, so that about 1 in. (2.5 cm) extends beyond each end. Thread a crimp bead onto the nylon filament above the coil and double the filament back through the crimp bead to form a loop. Squeeze the crimp bead tightly with your chain-nose pliers to secure it on the filament.

LEFT

These earrings are nothing more than an elongated spiral threaded with beads—one of the simplest designs in this book!

Christmas tree earrings

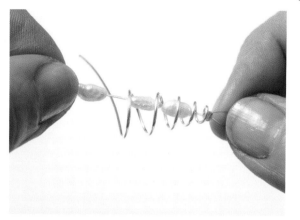

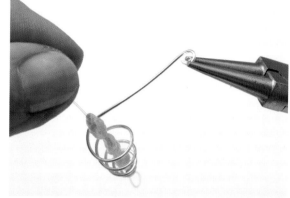

4 Thread the nylon filament inside the coil with freshwater pearls, right up to the last and widest coil.

5 Holding the filament firmly as you work, so that the beads cannot fall off, form a small circle at the end of the extending wire using the tips of your round-nose pliers.

6 Holding this circle firmly in your flat-nose pliers, spiral the wire around to form an open spiral that sits as a base to the tapered coil.

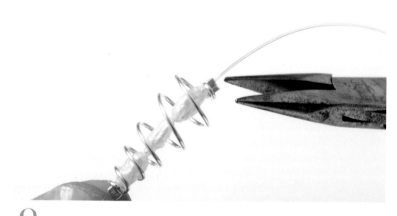

7 Thread the end of the nylon filament through the central circle of the base and feed on a crimp bead, pushing the crimp bead right up to the base of the spiral.

8 Squeeze the crimp bead with your chain-nose pliers to secure. Snip off any excess filament.

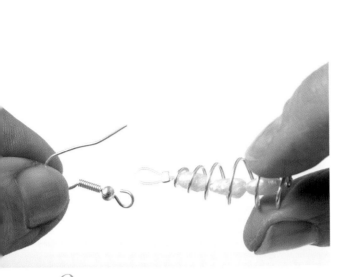

9 Repeat Steps 1–8 to make a second "tree." Attach the loop at the top of each "tree" to a ready-made ear wire.

ABOVE
A matching pearl and silver necklace looks both stylish and contemporary.

Variation

For a really festive-looking party piece, use Christmassy red and green beads. To make the matching necklace, make two tight spirals on the same piece of wire, one coiling in one direction and the other in another. Fold the wire in half so that one spiral sits on top of the other. When you stretch them out, as in Step 2 of the earrings, you will have a symmetrical cage, which you can thread with nylon and beads and attach to a chain or cord of your choice.

Suppliers

CGM Inc.
19611 Ventura Boulevard
Suite 211
Tarzana, CA 91356
Tel: (800) 426 5246
www.cgmfindings.com

Fire Mountain Gems
1 Fire Mountain Way
Grants Pass, OR 97526-2373
Tel: (800) 355 2137
www.firemountaingems.com

Jewelry Supply
Roseville
CA 95678
Tel: (916) 780 9610
www.jewelrysupply.com

Land of Odds
718 Thompson Lane
Ste 123, Nashville, TN 37204
Tel: (615) 292 0610
www.landofodds.com

Mode International Inc.
5111-4th Avenue
Brooklyn, NY 11220
Tel: (718) 765 0124
www.modebeads.com

Rings & Things
P.O. Box 450
Spokane, WA 99210-0450
Tel: (800) 366 2156
www.rings-things.com

Rio Grande
7500 Bluewater Road. NW
Albuquerque, NM 87121
Tel: (800) 545 6566
www.riogrande.com

Shipwreck Beads
8560 Commerce Place Dr. NE
Lacey, WA 98516
Tel: (800) 950 4232
www.shipwreckbeads.com

Stormcloud Trading Co.
725 Snelling Ave. N
St. Paul, MN 55104
Tel: (651) 645 0343
www.beadstorm.com

Studio Galli Productions
P.O. Box 14815
San Francisco, CA 94114
Tel: (408) 828 8350
www.studiogalli.tv
(DVDs only)

Thunderbird Supply Company
1907 W. Historic Rte. 66
Gallup, NM 87301
Tel: (800) 545 7968
www.thunderbirdsupply.com

www.americanbeads.com
(Online sales only)

Wig Jig
P.O. Box 5124
Gaithersburg, MD 20882
www.wigjig .com

CANADA

Abra-kad-abra Collection
763 Mont-Royal East Metro
Mont-Royal
Montreal (QC) H21-1W8
www. abra-kad-abra.com

Bead and Craft
   International Inc.
7357 Woodbine Avenue
Unit #1 Suite# 314
Markham (ON) L3R-6L3
Tel: 416-640-0168
www.beadandcraft.com

Bead Box Inc.
17-B Cartier Avenue
Pointe-Claire Village
Pointe-Claire (QC) H9A-1Y5
Tel: 514-697-4224
Fax: 697-3224
Email beadbox@bellnet.ca

The Beadery
446 Queen Street West
Toronto (ON) M5V-2A8
Tel: 416-703-4668
Fax: 703-3586
www.thebeadery.ca
Email: beads@thebeadery.ca

BeadFX Inc.
128 Manville Road, #9
Scarborough (ON) M1L 4J5
+1.877.473.BEAD (2323)
416.701.9182
www.beadfx.com

A Beauiful Gift
5460 Yonge Street, Suite 103
North York (ON) M2N-6K7
Tel: 416-226-5762
Fax: 647-436-1981
www.abeautifulgift.ca

Bedrock Supply
9435-63 Avenue
Edmonton (AB) T6E-0G2
Tel: 780-434-2040
Fax: 780-436-3294
www.bedrocksupply.ca

Canada Beading Supply
11A-190 Colonnade Road South
Ottawa (ON) K2E 7J5
Tel: (613) 727-3886
Fax: (613) 727-5637
www.canbead.com

Index

A

amethysts
  birthstone 69
  chips 6, 71
aquamarines, birthstone 69

B

bangles, flower 53–5
beaded bauble pendant 115–17
beaded scarf slide 48–51
beads 8, 12–13
  and size of wire 13
  sizes 13
  threading 14
birthdays 63–81
birthstone bracelet 66–9
birthstone necklace 71–3
birthstones 13, 65, 69
bow pin 61–3
bracelets
  birthstone 66–9
  flower cuff 53–5
  lover's knot 35–7
bridal hair grip 92–5
bride's tiara 84–7
bridesmaid's necklace 97–9
bridesmaid's wand 100–3

C

chain-nose pliers 10
chains
  Cupid's love 27–9
  made from jump rings 17
  ready-made 13, 74, 115
  wiggly 56–9
chips, semi-precious birthstones
  6, 69
Christmas 105–25
Christmas tree earrings 123–5
Christmas wreath necklace
  119–21
clasps
  beaded eye 22
  coiled fish-hook and fastener
    23

'eye' 20–1
fish-hook 18–19
ready-made 13
S-shaped 20
clips, tassel 74–7
closed spirals 16
copper wire 27
cord, for pendants 115, 121
crystals 89
  for birthstone 69
cuffs, flower 53–5
Cupid's love chain 27–9

D

diamonds, birthstone 69
doubled fish-hook clasp 18–19
dragonfly 83, 100–3

E

earrings
  Christmas star 109
  Christmas tree 123–5
  holly leaf 112
  lover's knot 37
  to match bridesmaid's
    necklace 99
  to match Cupid's love chain
    29
  to match pearly necklace 89,
    91
  to match Sweetheart
    necklace 31–2
emeralds, birthstone 69
ends, neatening 21

F

fasteners
  clasps and 23
  'eye' of 20–1
findings
  (ready-made components) 13
  chains 13, 74
  clip or key-ring 74
  lapel pins 79

fish-hook clasp 18
  coiled 22, 23
  doubled 18–19
flat-nose pliers 10
flower cuff 53–5
flower pin 79–81

G

garnets, birthstone 69
glass beads 12

H

hair grips, bridal 92–5
hammers 10–11
  for work hardening 19
head pins, making 15
heart shapes 27–9, 43–5
  beaded 30–3
  crystal 35–7
holly-leaf necklace 110–13

J

jump rings
  connecting with 17
  making 16–17

L

leather, for pendant cord 115
links, using jump rings 17
love eternal necklace 43–5
lover's knot bracelet 35–7
lover's ring 25, 38–41

M

mandrels 11
materials 11–13
Mother's Day 47–63

N

napkin rings
    Christmas wreath 118
    flower 53
necklaces
    birthstone 71–3
    bridesmaid's 97–9
    Christmas tree 125
    Christmas wreath 119–21
    holly-leaf 110–13
    love eternal 43–5
    pearly 89–91
    Sweetheart 30–3

O

opals, birthstone 69
open spirals 16

P

pearls 89
    birthstone 69
pearly necklace 89–91
pendants
    beaded bauble 115–17
    Christmas star 107–9

peridots, birthstone 69
pins
    bow 61–3
    flower 79–81
    head 15
pliers 10

R

rings, lover's 25, 38–41
round-nose pliers 10
rubies, birthstone 69

S

sapphires, birthstone 69
scarf slides, beaded 48–51
seed beads 12–13
semi-precious birthstones
    6, 13, 69
spirals, making 16
stakes, flat steel 11
star pendant, Christmas 107–9
Superglue, to fix clasps 23, 45
Sweetheart necklace 30–3

T

tassel clip 74–7
techniques 14–23
    making clasps 18–19, 20–1, 22
    making fasteners 20–1, 23
    making head pins 15
    making jump rings 16–17
    making spirals 16
    neatening ends 21
    threading beads 14
    work hardening 19
tiara, bride's 7, 84–7
tools 10–11
topaz, birthstone 69
turquoise, birthstone 66, 69

V

Valentine's Day 25–45

W

wand, bridesmaid's 100–3
weddings 83–103
wiggly chain 56–9
wire 11–12
    precious-metal 11–12
    thicknesses (gauges) 12
    threading beads 14
wire cutters 10
work hardening 19
wreaths, Christmas 119–21

Acknowledgments

Thank you to everyone who helped toward getting this book to publication, especially Cindy Richards, my publisher, who still has faith in my abilities, and Sarah Hoggett, who not only edits and advises but manages to decipher and translate my step-by-step text into something more palatable. Also, big thanks to Geoff Dann, who has added a luxurious elegance to all the photography of the pieces.